Retirement 101

Retirement 101

How TIAA-CREF Members Should Deal
with the Dramatic Changes in Their Pensions

WILLARD F. ENTEMAN

The University of Wisconsin Press

The University of Wisconsin Press
114 North Murray Street
Madison, Wisconsin 53715

3 Henrietta Street
London WC2E 8LU, England

Library of Congress Cataloging-in-Publication Data
Enteman, Willard F.
    Retirement 101: how TIAA-CREF members should deal with the dramatic
changes in their pensions / Willard F. Enteman.
    244 pp.   cm.
    Includes bibliographical references (pp. 219–220) and index.
    ISBN 0-299-13570-5 (cloth)   ISBN 0-299-13574-8 (paper)
    1. College teachers—United States—Retirement.   2. Universities and colleges
—United States—Faculty—Retirement.   I. Title.
LB2334.E58   1992
331.25'2—dc20   92-18510

This volume is dedicated to

faculty and academic staff,

past, present, and future

in gratitude

for

their dedication and contributions

to the past, present, and future.

Contents

Chapter 8: Late Retirement Planning and Death 162

Appendix: Personal Investment Management 185

Preface: An Academic Odyssey

This book is the result of one tack on a lifetime odyssey among disparate personal interests in philosophy, economics, and management. While my primary interest has always been in philosophy, the other interests have also been an important part of my life, and their diversity is reflected in my educational career. I majored in philosophy as an undergraduate, and that was a joyous selection. I was challenged intellectually in ways I would never have imagined. I also learned something about faculty in that process. As a freshman and sophomore, I was absorbed with the standard fare of adolescent distractions. Somehow through it all, the faculty went on teaching us what we would learn, though we must have seemed boorish at best. However, once I became a serious student with a genuine interest in the life of the mind, the faculty was there to challenge, prod, support, and celebrate that development. Looking back later, it was a wonder to me that this gathering of first-rate minds had the patience to wait out adolescence. From my undergraduate major in philosophy, I entered immediately into business school. It took a while to adjust to the subject matter and the renowned case method, but once the shakedown cruise was over, I found business school interesting and challenging. The courses were only disappointing when they tried to deal with philosophical topics, such as business ethics. Those discussions seemed to descend into something reminiscent of dormitory bull sessions.

As graduation from business school approached, I was thoroughly confused about my future career. Going to work in business seemed an obvious alternative, but I knew that if I did that, I would forever close the door marked Theory. At the same time, I was not sure I wanted to shut the door on practical issues either.

My wife and I were married between my two years in business school when both of us thought I was headed for business. (Those were the days when wives often shelved their personal ambitions in order to support their husbands in graduate school. In recognition, the business school offered what they called a Ph.T. degree to our wives. It stood for "Put Hubby Through." My wife was so indignant that she refused to attend the conferral ceremony. Thus, in 1961, began women's liberation in our family.) As my doubts about going into business began to grow, we talked and talked. Confused and inarticulate as I was, she somehow understood what was troubling me and why I thought I wanted to continue in graduate school toward a doctorate, and she was ready to continue supporting us.

The question then became, A doctorate in what? Business was a possibility. That might combine all the interests, but in the business school, deep theory did not seem to be of much interest even to the faculty. Economics seemed like a reasonable compromise, especially if I were to emphasize finance where my interests in theory, mathematics, logical analysis, and practical issues might come together. However, in 1961, economists had "religion." Learning economics reminded me more of youthful lessons in the catechism than of an intellectual search without prior commitments.

And then there was philosophy. There could be little question about deep theory, but there was plenty of question about maintaining a practical interest. I talked to everyone who would listen. The corner was turned one day when I discussed my dilemma with one of the business school professors I admired most. He said something like: "If you go ahead in business or economics, you will never return to philosophy, but if you go ahead in philosophy, you may return to business and economics." That did not end my dilemma, nor have those tensions been entirely resolved even to this day, but somehow it put into perspective the priorities I wanted to pursue. I graduated from business school that spring and two days later began my first graduate courses in philosophy. Once again, there was a period of adjustment, but it soon became clear to me that I had made the right decision.

I was able to maintain my interests in economics and business. I did some consulting and continued to read about business. The world of finance fascinated me and still does. Some people read novels, go to the movies, or watch television as a break from their regular commitments. I read prospecti, business cases, financial analyses, and economic reports. That is, after all, a break form the likes of Plato, Aristotle, Kant, and Wittgenstein.

Acquaintances have suggested that these interests of mine are in fundamental conflict and that my insistence on maintaining all of them is evidence of an intellectual, if not psychological, disorder. (When I was completing my Ph.D. and searching for a philosophy post, one of my professors suggested that I leave reference to my M.B.A. off my curriculum vita because it might be taken as a sign of a lack of seriousness in philosophy.) I have never tried to reply to the sceptics beyond saying that those *are* my interests, and that I do not wish to turn my back on any of them.

As a result of the interests, once I began my faculty career, I was something of an attractive nuisance for people who believed I should become an administrator. However, I resisted for many years. I was deeply engaged in my teaching and my research. Each time I was asked to consider an administrative post, I would remember my business school professor and tell myself that if I went into administration, I would never make it back to philosophy. However, the longer I remained as a faculty member, the more convinced I became that our colleges and universities had lost their sense of purpose and an appropriate sense of priorities. To put the matter too simplistically, I believe the ideal college or university is best described with the metaphor of a dedicated teacher on one end of a log and a student on the other end. The modern trend seems to me to overemphasize the log and underemphasize research and learning. For example, the expenditures devoted directly to the education of students make up a minor portion of the total expenditures in many of our colleges and universities. I finally decided to accept an offer to try my hand at administration.

My years as an academic administrator in a sense brought my interests together (and gave conclusive evidence to some that I lacked seriousness about philosophy). They were in many ways rich and rewarding years because I was able to use my diverse interests and attempt to help institutions return to their root purposes. I was also able to teach each semester and continue with a modest program of philosophical research. I told the presidents and boards for whom I worked that if there should be a conflict between my teaching and my administration, I would return to the classroom without expressing any regrets. I learned a great deal in my administrative life, not the least of which is that, along with the faculty, there is a cadre of academic staff devoted to the education of students and concerned about the institutional distractions posed by so many other forces. I also learned more about the retirement program for faculty and administrative staff than I would have known if I had remained in the classroom.

One of the most disturbing memories of my administrative career grew out of a self-imposed assignment. I was so grateful for the education which earlier professors had given me that I decided I wanted to talk with retired faculty and staff of institutions in which I was an administrator. The people I met were still deeply devoted to education. However, I realized that they were often living under economic circumstances which, to say the least, should have been embarrassing for institutions which thought of themselves as humane. Leaving aside the assignment of responsibility, I believed many of those people had been mistreated in regard to their retirement.

While I do not regret my time as an administrator, it was largely a failure from the perspective of the larger agenda which drove me there in the first place. The task of balancing budgets while keeping some semblance of concern with the education of students and the development of faculty was difficult, but not all that difficult. It was a little like a standard business school case. However, beyond solving the immediate crises of budgets, of conundrums posed by students, and of faculty promotion decisions, I wanted to work with my administrative and faculty colleagues to suggest systemic reconstruction of our institutions. I hoped to do that through rigorous planning, so that the implications of what we were doing would be clear. I could never accomplish that task. Gradually, I came to feel like Sisyphus. I would no sooner get the ball rolled partway up the hill than it would get shoved back down. Most of the time, those who did the shoving were members of boards which theoretically held the institution in trust. It took me a while to realize that if the center of legal responsibility did not want the institution to focus on education, I was at the wrong end of the lever for causing the change. Finally, I recognized that, unlike Sisyphus, I could make a choice. I could make it back from administration to philosophy because my personal center had always remained in philosophy. I knew there were other ways, both practical and theoretical, to follow my disparate interests. However, as I decided to return to the classroom and the library, the memory of those retired faculty and staff continued to haunt me.

While I have been in favor of the recent changes in our retirement provisions, I knew that as a result of the changes, there would be substantial opportunity for more mistreatment of faculty and academic staff. Concepts need to be changed, personal planning needs to be initiated, and some attention needs to be given to the technical aspects of retirement by each of us. However, there is no objective guidance which understands the new conditions of retirement for faculty and academic staff. My hope is that this book will provide that guidance. It is a place to start. It is not the place to stop. Each faculty member and academic staff member should now feel a high degree of responsibility for personal retirement planning. I hope the book may be used as a source which helps people ask good questions and pursue answers which may be relevant for their own situations. In writing the book, I have often been forced to choose between an emphasis on fundamental concepts and an emphasis on details. In my own view, it is the concepts which we need to understand most clearly now. I am convinced that once you understand the concepts, you will be able to discover the details and make the arrangements which are relevant to your special situation. While there is not much standard philosophy in this book, it is driven by the philosopher's interest in analyzing unexamined assumptions and in grounding action in appropriate concepts. Thus, on a personal, practical level, the book has brought my interests together. On other occasions, I hope to be able to take another tack and show how those diverse interests can also be brought together in a more theoretical and philosophical whole.

This book owes its existence to many people whom I want to acknowledge here. First, I wish to thank some people who shall by necessity remain anonymous. For a number of years, I have provided informal personal financial planning advice to many academics. They sought me out, and I have always been honored by their belief that I might help them on such a serious and important topic. Using a take-off on what will be called fee-only financial planning in chapter 2, I refer to myself as a "free-only" financial planner. I usually remind these friends that my father, who was a lawyer, used to say free legal advice is worth what is paid for it. Nevertheless, by their questions and confidence, they led me to study financial planning more deeply than I might have otherwise.

As a result of those discussions, I spent a portion of the academic year 1981–1982, investigating whether there was an opportunity for fee-only financial planning for faculty and academic staff. On the basis of my many conversations, I suspected that there was a genuine need, but I did not know whether there was sufficient recognition of the need. After reading extensively in the literature of financial planning, and after investigating the field itself, I came to the conclusion that there was not enough to warrant anything more than variations on my own invention of free-only financial planning. At that time, we had little effective choice. Our retirement planning was locked into TIAA-CREF. Our choices were very limited and only had to be made on one or two occasions. Nevertheless, if those anonymous people had not asked me to help them with their questions, I would not have learned what I have about this field, and this book would not have been possible.

I am indebted to President Carol Guardo, who understood my desire to stop pushing balls up hills and conclude my academic career in the classroom and the library. She graciously allowed me to return to my faculty post and helped me in the reentry process. I am also indebted to President Nazarian, Vice-President Salesses, and Dean Weiner of Rhode Island College for their help with my reentry and for their willingness to continue to push balls up hills after this weaker colleague gave up. In addition, I want to express my gratitude to Professor Howell as Chair of the Rhode Island College Philosophy Department and to my colleagues in the Department for their graciousness as this administrator returned to the "real world." I am also appreciative of the governing boards at both Eckerd College and the Hotchkiss School. They have restored my faith that lay academic boards can put education at the center.

I am indebted to many readers of earlier versions of this manuscript. John Secco helped me see how to make the manuscript more direct. Peter Kulis helped me with some of the analytical work. Alexander Astin forced me to remember the broader perspective which helped lift the sights of the project. Paul Helmreich gave one version of the manuscript the kind of rigorous and careful review which characterizes the commitment of an historian. Three people should be recognized especially. Jean Pearce, Patricia Marzzacco, and Eliot S. Knight read different versions of the manuscript with exquisite, detailed care and provided comment, and criticism. Their comments helped improve the manuscript in many ways.

I want to make special recognition of Katie, Sally, and David Enteman. It has not been easy for them to be associated with someone who could never seem to figure out what he wanted to do when he grew up. The stability of a loving family has allowed each of us to follow our own adventures and has given me the luxury of challenging assumptions.

I also want to express deep appreciation for the many teach-

ers and professors who have taught me from the earliest days
to the present. It has become something of a parlor game recently to take rhetorical shots at faculty and university staff.
None of us is above criticism which is well grounded and responsive to appropriate canons of research and investigation.
However, much that is being said bears more testimony to our
collective failure to do a better job of teaching the critics about
the requirements of logic than it does to the substance of their
arguments. Joe Nyquist used to call such rhetoric "conclusions
developed without fear of research." It must have some instant
gratification for the authors, for it obviously sells books and
op-ed pieces. In contrast to that fashionable line, I am glad to
take this opportunity to express appreciation to members of
academic staffs and to faculty members whose contributions
are much greater than their detractors would have the public
believe. Long after the politically motivated have gone to that
special circle Dante reserved for them, students will remember
their teachers.

On behalf of readers of this book, I want to express deep
appreciation to the University of Wisconsin Press. From the
outset of this project, I was concerned about how it might be
published. The financial world is a complex and interlocking
one. I wanted to be sure there would be neither the reality nor
the appearance of a conflict of interest. As a result, my preference was for a university press. However, I knew it would
take one with a willingness to venture into an unusual area.
I think the commitment of the staff at the University of Wisconsin Press to academic life made them realize they should
break past assumptions and consider this project. They have
been encouraging and helpful from the start.

In the spirit of what is called due diligence, I want to make
a disclaimer. This book is not sponsored by, supported by, or
a promotional piece for any financial services organization. I
believe it is important to be explicit on this issue because so
much of the material you will read about your retirement is, directly or indirectly, promotional material for financial services
organizations. There may be some places in the book where

you may wish I had made explicit reference to commercial organizations. However, I believed that if the book referred to some commercial organizations, there would be an appearance that perhaps in some insidious way it was supported by those organizations. Thus, I would not permit selective reference. I then faced a dilemma; I could either refer to all organizations or none. If I were to try to refer to all relevant organizations, even on a specific topic, I would almost surely leave some out. Not only is the domain enormous, but also it changes so rapidly that even during the publication preparation, there would be significant changes. That would lead us back to the problems of the appearance of bias in selectivity. I decided not to compromise and, thus, I refer to no financial services organizations by name, with one exception. The one exception is, of course, TIAA-CREF. I believe that efforts to avoid referring to TIAA-CREF by name would be entirely contrived. However, since I do refer to TIAA-CREF by name, I want to make an explicit disclaimer to the effect that this book is not sponsored by, supported by, or a promotional piece for TIAA or CREF. On the one hand, it is not a TIAA-CREF-bashing book. I do not find that a very productive approach for the improvement of our retirement. On the other hand, it is not a TIAA-CREF-advocacy book either. We can be assured people at TIAA-CREF will take care of their own advocacy. I hope readers will understand the need to refer directly to TIAA-CREF, and that they will conclude that the positions taken are advanced in the readers' interests, not the interests of any financial services organizations, including TIAA-CREF. My hope is to help readers take charge of this part of their world, which has changed so much.

In reviewing an earlier draft of the manuscript, Paul Helmreich accurately observed that a book of this nature could be written in such a way that the reader would be expected to read it all together, or it could be written on the assumption that readers would examine only those chapter(s) which were of most interest to them. Professor Helmreich argued that a successful manuscript could not have it both ways, and he challenged me to resolve the tension. Others will have to say how successfully I have met his challenge. As someone interested in planning in general, I am conscious of the fact that all the parts are interrelated. However, I recognize that certain parts will be more relevant at different times in a person's life. My suggestion is to read the entire book in order to understand the context and the general points, and then to read more carefully the sections of greatest interest.

Part One

Preliminary Issues

1

Orientation

The Revolution in Retirement Planning

It would be hard to exaggerate the impact of recent changes in retirement provisions for faculty members and other academic staff who have been covered by the Teachers Insurance Annuity Association and the College Retirement Equities Fund (TIAA-CREF). Without much preparation or warning, our retirement world has been turned upside down. Earlier assumptions need to be reexamined and reevaluated; what was once a subject to which we reasonably devoted only passing attention has become one that requires significantly greater attention. Where there was little discretion previously, there is now a very large range of choices. What was once an area largely beyond our control and managed *by* other people *for* us has become, as of March, 1990, one in which we must take responsibility for a wide range of decisions which may affect our future substantially.

One major change is known as *transferability*, which means that participants now have an opportunity to transfer their accumulated savings into investments which are not supervised by TIAA-CREF. The other change is known as *cashability*, which means that at retirement, participants have a right to receive the funds which have been accumulated to provide for their retirement, and they may use those funds in any way they wish. As a consequence, we have moved from a situa-

3

tion in which our choices were somewhere between minimal and none to one in which the choices are almost limitless. This book is designed to help faculty and academic staff ask the appropriate questions and make relevant decisions in regard to how they might exercise these new responsibilities. On the one hand, it proposes no simplistic solutions. On the other hand, it attempts to strip away the air of mystery in which this area often seems shrouded. I believe that, with a reasonable level of effort, we can take charge of these new responsibilities, and we can recognize various marketing efforts for what they are.

Until March of 1990, the gargantuan financial services industry could only look on jealously as TIAA-CREF grew to be the largest pension fund in the world, commanding more than $95 billion in assets, with a captive and largely docile membership of over one million members. The broader financial services industry had no way of gaining access to that potentially lucrative market. The introduction of transferability and cashability at once provides an opportunity for us, opens an enormous new market for the financial services industry, and converts TIAA-CREF from a paternalistic monopoly to a corporation under competitive pressures.

It seems clear that the financial services industry is starting to stir. The recent increase of their advertising in *The Chronicle of Higher Education* reveals their willingness to support their interest with resources. The financial services organizations still do not know how to approach the market, but they will continue to try. Almost surely, they will throw money at the problem until they find the solution. Compared to the tens of billions of dollars in assets at stake, hundreds of thousands of dollars spent in marketing will be seen as unimportant. As they say on the farm, even a blind pig will eventually find its food if you show it where the pen is.

If retirement planning were a science (which it surely is not), we would suggest in terminology reminiscent of the historian of science, Thomas Kuhn, that what has happened is a case of a scientific revolution and a paradigm shift. The reasons would be those suggested by Kuhn. It is not that some details have shifted in some marginal ways; rather, the entire conceptual structure of retirement for academics has gone through revolutionary change.

From the days of Andrew Carnegie's generous philanthropy until March, 1990, faculty retirement funding was fundamentally paternalistic. Initially it was to be provided by Carnegie's personal endowment. When that proved to be inadequate, it was conceived of as being provided by the contributions of institutions in the name of individual participants, which were held initially by TIAA alone and later by CREF also. All apart from the source or location of accumulation, the assumption remained that funds were provided *for* participants by a generous university and supervised in the interests of participants by a benevolent corporation. The major choices lay with TIAA-CREF and with each college or university through separate contracts with TIAA-CREF. Participants had a very limited range of choices designed to insure that they would be unlikely to make any decisions which might do them or their families irreparable harm.

Since March, 1990, colleges and universities continue to make contributions to a retirement fund. Increasingly, however, we shall be constrained only by law as to what we may do with *our* retirement savings. The paternalism of the previous system has been effectively eliminated. The new conceptual approach presumes first that during employment, the retirement accumulation is ours to manage according to our personal needs, and second that upon retirement, we can and should make our own decisions about how best to provide for our own retirement.

The new opportunity allows people to tailor the use of their funds to their personal needs. Until March of 1990, the only way we could receive a return of the funds which had been accumulated in our name was by purchasing a TIAA-CREF annuity. Participants could not receive their money in a lump sum even if their personal circumstances recommended against purchasing an annuity, nor could they use the money to purchase an annuity from another insurance company, even if that company provided a better annuity for them.

In their recent book on the professoriate, written shortly before the changes mentioned took place, Bowen and Schuster identify three major areas of potential change in what they call the faculty contract:

1. Prospective changes in mandatory retirement provisions
2. Prospective changes in the starting age for unreduced Social Security benefits
3. Prospective changes in the TIAA-CREF provisions

When they wrote their book, the changes in TIAA-CREF were only in the talking stage, and Bowen and Schuster said of them,

> A third area of change relates to the increasing restiveness of a minority of faculty and other higher education personnel concerning the investment, administration, and even use of retirement funds. . . . Some individuals claim that elements of the retirement system constitute unwarranted paternalism—that they should have wide latitude in choosing their investments and complete freedom to switch funds among them and to withdraw their capital accumulation in a single sum at termination.[1]

They also make a concrete suggestion about what needs to be done in the face of these prospective changes:

> . . . expert retirement counseling should be available to faculty members. As they approach retirement, the counseling should inform them about the features of the plan in which they are enrolled and apprise them of the possibilities and options connected with their retirement annuities.[2]

Even in this wise and prescient judgment, however, Bowen and Schuster did not foresee how dramatic the change would be. If we wait until we approach retirement to begin thinking seriously about our retirement provisions, we shall find that our alternatives will be substantially reduced.

All three of the changes Bowen and Schuster speculated

about have now taken place, and they promise to have a substantial impact on the financial conditions of our retirement.
At the time of Bowen and Schuster's book, mandatory retirement for tenured faculty members was still legal. It is under review now, and in this book I assume that mandatory retirement
will be dropped as a feature of faculty employment. Substantial
social security changes are also taking place. If those were the
only changes, I would have described them as evolutionary and
not revolutionary. It is the introduction of transferability and
cashability which makes the changes truly revolutionary, for
it places responsibility directly on our shoulders, and it forces
us to be directly involved with retirement planning for ourselves over the bulk of our career. We should not wait until we
"approach retirement" as Bowen and Schuster say; retirement
planning must go on throughout our career.

Bowen and Schuster's call for expert retirement counseling is appropriate and even more necessary now than it was
when the alternatives under TIAA-CREF were minimal. That
advice must be untainted by any conflict of interest, because
the stakes will be very high for us. There will be a plethora of
supposedly free sources of advice, but there are good reasons
to suggest that we take their advice with caution.

In general, we shall find ourselves on an uncomfortable cusp.
We shall have access to enough discretionary funds to be a target for the financial services industry, but we shall not have
the resources to retain the phalanx of lawyers, accountants,
investment managers, estate planners, and so on who provide
their services to more wealthy people. By way of analogy, we
will find that our situation with regard to retirement planning
is similar to the one we face when we send our children to
college: we have enough personal resources to disqualify our
children for scholarships, but we do not have enough to pay for
their education without substantial financial disruption. The
only solution is careful planning.

Thus, this book has several purposes: (1) to alert faculty and
academic staff to their new responsibilities, (2) to make them
aware that they will become targets for aggressive marketing

programs, and (3) to help them move from being passive recipients with little choice to being active consumers who use their freedom to make effective choices. I shall suggest questions we should ask and decisions we must make in regard to our retirement under the restructured system.

Disconnectedness versus Control

In all retirement planning, the prospective retiree must deal with a particular source of tension. On the one hand, we have the vision of people who wish to retire and never think about anything more challenging than when to play golf. Such people need an ample source of income that requires no thought or question of its adequacy. To use my terminology, they want to be disconnected from financial issues. On the other hand, we have the vision of people who supposedly retire but continue at the same pace and under the same demands as before. Since they now have the time, such people may become even more involved in their own personal financial affairs and may spend most of their time talking with their brokers and financial advisers. Presumably, whether by necessity or choice, most of us fall somewhere in between those two extremes. Most of us are not wealthy enough to ignore our financial situation; consequently, we must pay some attention to it whether we want to or not. On the other hand, many of us, perhaps especially academics, would not find retirement attractive if we had to spend all our waking hours reading stock quotations.

I shall assume here that academics feel about these issues basically as I do: I applaud the freedom which we have now, and I dislike the patronizing paternalism which defined the old system. Whether or not I wish to do anything different with my freedom, I am glad more alternatives are available to me and my colleagues. At the same time, I cannot help expressing some nostalgia for the old days. Basically, as a scholar and teacher, I would like to be disconnected from the need to concern myself with money. I suspect that I have greater

tolerance for reading documents like prospecti, insurance contracts, trust instruments, investment analyses, and IRS Codes
than many of my academic colleagues, but even my tolerance
is limited.

I assume faculty are themselves caught in the tension between wanting to be in control and wanting to be disconnected
from such matters. We must all find our places on that spectrum. Some will naturally lean more to one end than to the
other. Those who wish to return to the old days can confine
themselves to the previous provisions of TIAA-CREF. They
might read this book just to be sure that nothing in particular
deserves their direct attention, for it deals with issues which
transcend even the changes discussed thus far. At the other
end of the spectrum will be some who want to actively manage all aspects of their retirement planning on a regular and
continual basis. This book will be too superficial for them; I
designed it for academics who would rather think about other
things, but who recognize that in the new circumstances require more personal involvement. After all, most of us mow
our own lawns, and only a few of us actually enjoy doing it.

Presumptions of the Book

The book presumes first that the transition to retirement is primarily a gradual one in which we can identify stages for analysis. Second, it presumes that some irreversible events occur in
our lives, and that we must take account of them as we plan for
the future. Finally, the book presumes that the application of
intelligence to this topic will prove useful, and that we should
be personally involved in planning for the future.

However, the book does provide some nonspecific guidance
which I hope will be useful. I refer to such guidance sometimes as generalizations, rebuttable assumptions, or guiding
principles. I am constantly aware that our lives are unique and
composed of special circumstances. As far as I can discover, all
rules for retirement planning have substantial exceptions. The

generalizations should provide a context for asking good questions and developing specific plans for specific conditions. In suggesting that we now face a new world and must be ready to assume active responsibility, the book attempts to provide generalizations, rebuttable assumptions, and guiding principles which will help you accept this responsibility. They are not, however, a substitute for responsibility.

Among the generalizations, I make some presumptions about the various phases in the careers and personal lives of faculty and academic staff, and it will be helpful to identify those phases.

Phases in Career and Personal Life

The initiation of a career is also the beginning of the preparation for retirement, whether or not that career is in education. We proceed from appointment to retirement continuously. There are milestones along the way, and there are phases which can be analytically distinguished, but basically it is a gradual process, like the maturation of children. There is no question after the children have turned twenty-one that they are not the infants we cradled, but it is difficult to identify the changes on a day-by-day basis. As each day goes by, the changes are not obvious, but they have nevertheless occurred.

Now that the responsibilities and the choices have been given to us, we shall need to begin thinking about retirement almost from the start. As we move through our careers, the questions and the decisions will be different, but the need for planning will remain constant.

In accordance with the gradual transition process, the book is divided into four parts. This first part discusses preliminary issues which need to be addressed in order to understand retirement planning in general. The preliminaries are lengthy because, given the circumstances, I have assumed that participants in TIAA-CREF are unfamiliar with the topic itself. Under TIAA-CREF's earlier approach, we were prevented from exercising fundamental alternatives, so it made little sense to consider them. Thus, I assume there is little familiarity with the very broad range of alternatives which now face the participants and that, if anything, the range of alternatives is likely to broaden in the future.

Parts 2, 3 and 4 follow roughly the course of a participant's career. I have not put precise times on the occurrence of those divisions because there are too many variables. However, as a rough division, each part represents about twenty years. That will, of course vary widely. People who start their academic careers late will have to make appropriate adjustments, as will those who wish to retire early. However, academics typically begin their careers in their late twenties and approach retirement in their late sixties. This division should be close enough for individual adjustments. I want to emphasize that the very nature of the general retirement plan under which we are covered—a so-called defined-contribution program—means that we should be active from the beginning.

Special mention should be made in this transition time of people who will be caught in the transition. Many people who are currently well along in their careers will have operated under the old system and now find themselves in a radically different system. They may be tempted to think that since I emphasize early planning, there is little they can do. However, the new system does provide them with important new opportunities, and they should consider them carefully. They will have to make the appropriate adjustments for their circumstances as they read, but since I am also in their position, I have been conscious of them in writing the book.

Part 2 discusses decisions which should be addressed during the early phases of the participant's career. The issues are neither extensive nor overwhelming. At the same time, if decisions are delayed until they *must* be made, the range of alternatives may be unnecessarily limited.

Part 3 discusses intensive and extensive decisions which we must make as we approach retirement and prepare for it. That is the central part of the book, for it is during that period especially that the future success of the retirement is established, and it will not be easy to reverse decisions or nondecisions which have been made during that period.

Part 4 examines decisions which are made during the retirement years in order to insure their success.

As I pointed out previously, this division into parts is somewhat arbitrary. Throughout the book, there is an emphasis on the need for total retirement planning. I suggest that regardless of the particular stage you are in, you should be familiar with the entire book, so that you can put actions in an appropriate context.

Finally, there is a chapter-length appendix which discusses the specific topic of actively managing your financial assets. Such active management is a topic of continuing interest throughout the various phases, not specifically in a particular phase. There are alternatives to active management, and there is no presumption here that people should actively manage their assets. I feared that if the appendix were in the main body of the book, its size alone would leave an impression of how I thought people should respond to these opportunities. However, if the material in the appendix were not included, then the suggestion to consider active management would be empty because readers would have no guidance. Finally, it seems that some people may wish to do some of both. For example, those who continue to use TIAA-CREF as the sole manager of their retirement savings may have other assets which need to be managed but cannot be part of their TIAA-CREF account. As it is, I do not suggest the direct purchase of stocks, bonds, options, and so forth. I suggest indirect investment through mutual funds. The appendix is intended to provide some guiding principles for making decisions about those investments.

All retirees face two great fears. One is that they will run out of money before they die. The other is that a debilitating illness will leave them physically and fiscally wrecked. This material on retirement planning is designed to help moderate both those fears. I know of no way to remove all fear of fiscal inadequacy; however, a combination of control, flexibility, knowledge, and planning should enable us to moderate that fear as much as possible. I also discuss alternatives designed to moderate the fear of physical debilitation. There are no magical answers here, either, and it is inevitable that the human body will deteriorate with advancing age. However, we can take a number of steps to help with the financial burdens imposed by that deterioration, and they should give us a greater sense of control and flexibility. As with the fiscal matters alone, planning is critically important. As the years go by, alternatives are cut off, and if we delay too long, decisions will eventually have to be made on someone else's timetable and at someone else's pace. The area of medical care is linked with the area of fiscal care, and the issues should be considered jointly.

The final phase of retirement planning involves the approaching death of the retiree. Death is a fact of life and a fact of retirement planning, which should include planning for the disposition of assets after death.

While the Berlin Wall surrounding TIAA-CREF has been largely torn down, and the lingering paternalistic attitudes of TIAA-CREF and college and university authorities are being substantially eroded, there may be some backsliding, and we should remember that TIAA-CREF made these changes only reluctantly and under a great deal of pressure. We remain in a world of buck-passing in which university authorities prohibit some actions because they say TIAA-CREF does not allow them, and TIAA-CREF authorities prohibit them because they say they are not authorized in the university contract with TIAA-CREF (and both occasionally declare that the real problems are federal legislation, state legislation, or the IRS). There is still a political agenda. Even if we do not personally imagine a condition in which we might exercise an added element of flexibility and control, I believe the alternatives should be made available to others.

Irreversible Events

A number of events in our lives are effectively irreversible. They are exceptions to the general approach established in the previous section of a smooth and gradual transition from one phase to another. To a significant degree, we may control some of these events; others are essentially beyond our control. It is important to note these events because of the way in which they interrupt the transitory process, and because once they have occurred, our lives will have changed irreversibly.

■ *Tenure* The major event which is essentially irreversible in the early career of a faculty member is the achievement of tenure. While failure to achieve tenure may have a substantial negative financial impact, it has only a marginally positive impact when it does occur. This is not a book on tenure, nor is it a book about how to obtain tenure. Nevertheless, tenure looms so large in the life of faculty members that it cannot be ignored. While the failure to achieve tenure may not be absolutely irreversible in the career of a faculty member, it is as close as most would like to come to an irreversible negative event. A faculty member who does not achieve tenure and leaves academe must make decisions with regard to his or her accumulated retirement funds; those decisions are discussed later.

■ *Retirement Timing* With the end of mandatory retirement provisions for tenured faculty, the timing of retirement is more in their hands. Early retirement schemes may continue to be presented to faculty, but as universities face increasingly constrained markets of qualified faculty, early retirement schemes may fade, and more incentives may be created to persuade faculty to continue teaching beyond the so-called normal retirement age of sixty-five. However, once the decision to retire has been made, a university is unlikely to allow its reversal, and so many actions follow actual retirement, that reversing it is a little like attempting to put toothpaste back in a tube. Deciding on a retirement date should involve consideration not only of the financial dimensions supplied by the institution, but also of the implications for the use of retirement savings, social security, medical coverage, and so forth. All these dimensions need to be integrated into a coherent retirement plan which specifies an advantageous date. In the past, the retirement date was imposed, and many people essentially backed into retirement timing. Now that we have much more control over the timing, it is a factor which we must take into account. Some distinction should probably be made between faculty members and other academic staff in regard to retirement timing. While, *de jure* mandatory retirement has not applied to academic staff in recent years, their employment conditions in general have led to a strong sense of *de facto* mandatory retirement for them. In addition, the increasing turnover of senior administrators and micromanagement by lay or political governing boards means that academic staff have less protection from pressures to retire. However, both faculty and academic staff need to think about *their* preferences for a retirement date even if the actual date may be a subject of some negotiation.

■ *Annuities* One of the most important aspects of annuities that participants must understand under the new conditions is that they are essentially irreversible. Once you have signed an annuity contract, there is basically no going back, no matter what new circumstances subsequently arise. From the insurance company's point of view, the irreversibility is understandable. If the company allowed us to withdraw after signing up for an annuity, its group projections would not be reliable. Suppose you were to sign up for an annuity program at age sixty-five, and a year later you found that you had a terminal disease which gave you a 50 percent chance of dying in the next six months. You might wish you had not signed up for the annuity, and you might want to get back everything but what had been paid out thus far. However, the basis of your annuity contract was that on average half of the people who reach age sixty-five will live for approximately seventeen more years. That took into account the fact that some would die in the first year and others would live for another thirty-four or more years.

Since the annuity contract is irreversible, you should think about it carefully and be sure to explore alternatives, so that you can make a sensible decision in the context of your own circumstances. A decision not to sign an annuity contract is always reversible. In this area alone, the change from the previous TIAA-CREF provisions is most radical. Previously, the TIAA-CREF participant could only choose among annuity options offered by TIAA-CREF. No other alternatives could be elected no matter how appropriate they might be for individual participants.

■ *Housing* Decisions about housing are also essentially irreversible, and you need to think about them carefully in order to coordinate them with other decisions which you must make about retirement. If you decide to sell your house and move into an apartment, you are unlikely to be able to buy that house—or any other—again. If you sell your house in order to move to a lifetime care community or in order to move into a custodial arrangement in a nursing home, you will have made a move which is, to all intents and purposes, irreversible.

■ *Health Care Provisions* There is a great temptation to evade decisions about health care provisions as long as possible. While abstractly we do not think we are immortal or shielded from the ailments of aging, it is easy to fool ourselves into thinking that since last year went by with no catastrophic medical problems, the next year will go by similarly. However, this is another case in which induction fails us. Turkeys who decide that the farmer, who feeds them well and keeps their pen clean, must be a true turkey supporter have not heard about Thanksgiving. Few people go through life with no serious illnesses and then suddenly die in their sleep one night. Most of us will suffer from some debilitating illness and die in an institutional setting. If you allow too much time to pass before making some provisions for your medical care in retirement, you may have some medical problems which will make you uninsurable and severely constrain your future alternatives. At the same time, if you elect to be part of a long-term medical plan when you are still healthy, you will also have made irreversible decisions which may have a significant financial impact. When long-term medical care plans are more than a sham, they are expensive (and I believe even some which are expensive are also a sham). Once again, planning is critical even if action is delayed.

■ *Death* Here is the classic irreversible event. While its timing may be beyond the reach of those who do not commit suicide, you can make plans which will go some distance toward defining the context of your life when you die and the impact on other people after your death. The thoughtful person will want to consider the various implications of the issues surrounding death.

Planning Is Critical in New Circumstances

Now that we have significant alternatives for our retirement years, planning is critical if those years are not going to be frustrating and a source of constant second-guessing. Fortunately, the burden of planning is not as great as it might appear to be at first. The issues themselves are not beyond the reach of any liberally educated person.

Liberal Education and Retirement Planning

In many ways, retirement planning for academics calls on the skills which we associate with good liberal education. We need to apply to our own personal needs what we have been teaching our students about liberal education. It is important to learn to ask the right questions, to learn the facts, and to insist on rational and judicious answers. The issues are serious, and we need to take this topic as seriously as we would other areas of scholarly concern. In fact, all the scholarly canons which we teach apply to this area and may be used. However, the content of this area is neither as profound nor as extensive as that of a standard academic discipline. This book attempts to give you sufficient background to do your own retirement planning, though at times it will make sense to seek outside objective help.

Objectivity and Language

As noted, it seems predictable that we shall become a target for substantial marketing efforts in the future. The cleverness of such efforts should not be underestimated, and there is little doubt that some will be disguised to look as if they are providing thoughtful and objective advice when they are actually selling a product or a line of products.

In this context, I discussed in the preface my decision to forgo reference to any financial service organizations except TIAA-CREF. I hope a fair reading of this book will reveal that it provides neither an automatic endorsement of nor an automatic deprecation of TIAA-CREF or any of its services. TIAA-CREF has become one among many corporations offering financial services to us. We should consider it along with the others on the basis of its ability to help us accomplish our objectives. I know there is a price to be paid for my puritanical stand. The approach I have chosen will put a greater burden on you, but I presume you are accustomed to doing research, and you will soon find that there are many sources of sponsored advice. We are all indebted to our librarian colleagues, and I am sure they will be helpful in orienting you to the literature which deals with these topics. Some college or university libraries may not have reference collections in this area because of the special mission of the institution and the library within it. However, librarians I know are more than cooperative about developing small collections which are of particular interest. In addition, public libraries often have good reference collections for these topics. The subject of gaining advice is examined in more depth in chapter 2.

Another characteristic of this area is its tendency to use euphemisms, jargon, and (bad) puns. Only the hairdressing profession seems more prone to cute expressions designed to evade reality. The attempts at rhetorical evasion are most pronounced when the topic is death. From *life* insurance to Funeral *homes*, death is a topic which is not to be raised (except by salespeople, who may use it as a cudgel in sales presentations). If you have watched the PBS television show "Wall Street Week," you know that apparently Louis Rukeyser has never heard a pun he does not like. Certainly, these topics do not need to be treated in a humorless fashion, but I presume that we appreciate some sophistication in our humor and that, even though we are often accused of using jargon, we do not approve of it except as necessary, which is not often. I also presume that we can face the facts of aging, sickness, and death without hiding behind euphemisms. Obviously, we shall have to learn the euphemisms and jargon of the trade in order to understand *their* language, but I shall try to explore the topics in straightforward terms.

Another aspect of general retirement planning is its assumptions about the characteristic audience being addressed. Somehow, in spite of recent social changes, the dominant imagery of the literature is that people are in familial settings which include a husband, who is on a payroll, a wife, who is not, and children who need some financial provisions. In addition, a typical assumption is that wives are blissfully ignorant of such masculine topics as financial affairs and, furthermore, that they could not understand the complicated mathematics even if they did become interested. Still further, the literature often assumes that the husband will predecease the wife, and that some provisions should be made for her unless she should remarry, in which case the provisions should be for the children. All of these assumptions are somewhat surprising to me because I have spent considerable time and energy educating women to take their places as fully participating and educated members of society, and yet the old concepts seem to retain their hold.

If the literature has taken into account any recent social changes, they have not been those which have brought increased respect for women, but those related to the increasing prevalence of divorce. Since the primary reader is presumed to be male, the literature assumes some protection is required to be sure previous wives do not get their hands on any more(!) money, that the most recent wife is cared for, that provisions are made for children from earlier marriages, and that there are contingencies in case the current marriage should end in divorce.

I evade all these issues of complex familial and other personal circumstances because the variations are overwhelming. Fundamentally, I address this book to individuals who need to plan for their retirement. Reference to a spouse is sometimes unavoidable (as in joint ownership by the entirety, for example), but my approach is directed at individuals developing plans in the belief that they can and will take into account the interests, needs, and desires of relatives and friends. I give some attention to double-income families, since they are becoming more prevalent—even financially necessary—in academia, but the primary focus is on individuals who will decide how to integrate their plans with the plans of others as appropriate. It should be obvious that where more than one retirement is to be planned, appropriate questions should be raised about the joint efforts. However, I cannot anticipate the nature of the retirement programs for people who are friends and relatives of those of us who have been covered by TIAA-CREF. The reader will need to learn about alternative programs where relevant, and take those consequences into account.

In the context of the presumptions explained in the previous paragraph, calculations presented in this book assume a unisex basis. For example, in discussing the actuarial calculations of life expectancy, it is common for some organizations (including TIAA-CREF) to make differentiations based on gender. Those differentiations are not included in this book. My suspicion is that over time, the data for the genders will converge. In addition, once we begin to categorize, there is no real reason to stop. Data for life expectancy is generated by geographic region, by religious preference, by race, by occupation, and so forth, and under some circumstances, those factors show greater statistical variance than that of gender. It would be excessively cumbersome to make all those differentiations. In addition, attempting to make such discriminations would give an illusion of precision to the book which is inappropriate.

The world of retirement planning is modestly confusing, but it is not beyond the grasp of liberally educated people. However, most of us are like other professionals who have a tendency to ignore our own personal lives in order to fulfill self-imposed professional demands. The lessons of liberal education and critical thinking will prove to be adequate, but a profession which demands sacrifice and helping others can attract to it just those people who tend to ignore their own future while they help others. We can no longer afford to assume that some benevolent organization(s) will take care of our future for us. Having understood the revolutionary changes in the conditions of our retirement, and having established the conditions and assumptions of this book, we are ready to turn to the active process of retirement planning.

2

Sources of Advice

Introduction

While there is no doubt that we can acquire the requisite knowledge to operate effectively in the area of retirement planning, few of us are likely to take time from professional obligations in order to become fully knowledgeable. In addition, we shall be offered a considerable amount of supposedly free advice from a number of sources. That advice may provide some useful information, and it should not be rejected completely. Nevertheless, such free advice is usually offered primarily because someone hopes to gain from those who follow it. This chapter presents discussion and analysis of the numerous sources of advice which are available, so that you can recognize their strengths and weaknesses.

There are three criteria for trustworthy advice: It should be objective, expert, and individualized. Following the last section of the previous chapter, it is tempting to go off on a lengthy tangent at this point about objectivity. The term has been subjected to a considerable amount of scholarly debate, and some believe it to be a permanently elusive goal, if not an incoherent one. In the context of this book, the term signifies "no conflict of interest." I do not expect an automobile salesperson to give me objective advice about whether the automobiles he sells are inferior to automobiles his competitors sell. However, I do expect something approaching "objective advice" when I read *Consumer's Reports* on automobiles.

Commission-Based Salespeople

When Arthur Miller wrote *Death of a Salesman*, people who were salesmen were called openly by that name (and they were essentially all males). Since then, especially in the financial services areas, euphemisms abound for what was a reasonably clear job title. Salespeople may call themselves financial consultants, financial counselors, customer service representatives, financial advisors, and so on. (Those who are called financial planners are discussed in the final section of this chapter.) Whatever their new titles, many of these former salespeople work on a direct commission basis. They are unlikely to suggest that you avoid using products on which they earn a commission, even if you should. Mutual fund salespeople would be delighted to persuade you to withdraw your retirement funds from TIAA-CREF and invest them all in one or more of the funds they sell. After all, they will receive a substantial commission based on that transaction. You should not be surprised that they are willing to spend a considerable amount of time trying to persuade you to make the move. Similar comments may be made about life insurance salespeople, stockbrokers, and so forth. In addition, it is useful to realize that these financial service areas are no longer as distinct as they once were, and you may find one person ready to represent—and collect commissions on—multiple services.

Awareness of salespeople's interest in commissions does not mean that one should never talk with them. They supply considerable amounts of information, and they are often happy to tailor a program specifically for you in order to get the account. Look and examine, but recognize that in the end it is your decision.

Salary-Based Salespeople

Neither in financial services nor in other areas do salespeople —whatever their moniker—work only on direct commission. Some are on salary but are nevertheless beholden to an employer and expected to promote the employer's products and services. For example, bank trust officers are not typically paid on a commission basis, but they are expected to represent their bank's services and to persuade financially attractive prospective customers to use them. Putting people on commission is one way to market services; corporations which pay their salespeople a salary have merely selected a different way to market their services.

Almost surely, part of the annual evaluation of salary-based salespeople will focus on their ability to attract and hold valued customers. In addition, their bonuses, which may be substantial, are likely to be based in part on successful customer relations. These people can be a source of considerable information, but the potential for a conflict of interest is also present in this area.

Some consumers prefer salary-based salespeople to commission-based salespeople. They often complain that commission-based salespeople ignore them after the initial transaction, which is probably true in some circumstances. Unless commission-based salespeople think you are a prospect for more commissions, they may wish to spend their time on what they call "live" prospects. Such consumers argue that the salaried person will always be there to answer questions and concerns. There is some truth in this view of commission-based salespeople versus salary-based salespeople. At the same time, we have all had experiences with large bureaucracies of people on salary who are more interested in getting home on time than in giving service.

Specific mention should be made of TIAA-CREF services in this regard. In a sense, we could assume that TIAA-CREF employees are like other salaried salespeople. However, TIAA-

CREF has had such a long history of serving educational and research institutions that it seems appropriate to give it special consideration. In the past, TIAA-CREF has provided considerable information to its members, including information relating to their own personal accounts. It has maintained toll-free lines, and it has been responsive to members' requests. It provides numerous written documents about general topics of interest to members. In its latest annual report, TIAA-CREF announced plans to introduce a program called LIFE Stages, which it says will provide educational programs for members, addressing their needs at different times in their careers.[1] Certainly, there is good reason to take advantage of these services.

At the same time, we must acknowledge that TIAA-CREF is entering into a very competitive marketplace. In a recent article in *The Chronicle of Higher Education*, an Executive Vice-President of TIAA-CREF is quoted as referring to the fact that they now have competitors.[2] A later article reported that the General Secretary of the AAUP took exception to some governance procedures in TIAA-CREF. Robert Atwell, whom the article identifies as a Trustee of CREF, is quoted as responding, "This [i.e., TIAA-CREF] is a business; it's not a faculty committee."[3] Mr Atwell is also the President of the American Council on Education, which is the umbrella organization for higher education in Washington. These quotes reveal that TIAA-CREF is, as stated, a business with none of the protection from competition it had previously. Some participants now have a wide range of choices, and they may decide to take some of their business elsewhere. Representatives of TIAA-CREF are not likely to suggest that members withdraw from TIAA-CREF and use other financial services, whether or not that is in the best interests of those members. Thus, its advice is worth considering, but it is not impartial, and we cannot afford to assume that TIAA-CREF will always give the best advice to a particular individual.

It would be a mistake to think that just because TIAA-CREF is a nonprofit corporation, its executives will not pursue its interests. After all, Blue Cross and Blue Shield are nonprofit organizations also, but they are quite capable of pursuing their primary interests aggressively.

University Benefits Counselors

For better or worse, the days are gone in which a president or dean would know each of us and, without access to files, clerks, and computer-based data files, would know our teaching schedules, research activities, campus responsibilities, and our compensation and professional plans. The days are gone, also, in which we can discuss our professional lives with the president or dean and receive in turn information about whatever arrangements the institution might make, along with advice from someone whose primary concern is our welfare. Even if modern presidents or deans had those intentions, and even if they were likely to remain in office long enough to establish close, confidential relationships with us, the conditions themselves have become so technical and legalistic that they could not fill the role.

As personnel issues have become more complicated, many universities have created personnel departments to administer relations between the institution and its employees. Within the personnel departments, they have created benefits offices, because benefits programs are technically personnel programs. Benefits officers can be a very useful source of information for us as we plan for retirement. It makes sense to take advantage of their knowledge and advice. It also makes sense to be conscious of the limits within which they work.

First, they have only a limited window on the total retirement planning scene. While benefits are an important aspect of retirement planning, many other factors must be taken into account. Second, benefits officers on university staffs have to be careful about what they say and what advice they give. For example, they should *not* give us advice about how to handle our retirement savings, because the university might be liable for a bad decision based on such advice. The benefits officer should, at most, outline some of the alternatives which we face. In that regard, benefits officers can supply important information, and you are well advised to take advantage of it, but they cannot be expected to develop an entire planning approach for you, and you cannot rely upon them for advice about many of the decisions which you must make.

General Literature

Material which deals with retirement planning may appear under that topic or it may be found encased within more general material on personal financial planning. While that literature is worth examination, as far as I am aware, none of it addresses the specific situation which we face after the changes in TIAA-CREF provisions. Much of the literature presumes that the retiree is on what is called a *defined-benefit plan*, whereas we are on what is called a *defined-contribution plan*. While it is not important to know a great deal about the differences between the two kinds of plans, they are substantial, and an overview of their differences will illustrate further the nature of our kind of retirement program.

Defined-Benefit Versus Defined-Contribution Plans

In a defined-benefit retirement program, the pension which will be paid to the retiree is defined by taking into account years of service to the company to arrive at some percentage of an average of some previous year's salaries. For example, consider a person who has worked at a company for the maximum number of years to justify the highest percentage. It is common for many retirement planners to assume that retirees will need only two-thirds of the comparable annual income they had before retirement. The plan, then, might establish that a pension will be two-thirds of the average of the salaries of the three years before retirement. That pension will continue for the lifetime of the retiree (there may be provisions for a beneficiary). If, for example, the average annual salary of the last three years of employment had been $48,000, then the lifetime pension would be $32,000 per year. (The calculations are more complicated, in part because some take into account social security payments as part of the estimated two-thirds, and others do not.)

The pension is an obligation first of the pension fund of the company and second of the company itself if there is not enough money in the fund. Under recent legislation (ERISA), the company is required to create a fund with an actuarially determined amount of money to support the pensions which are its obligations. Assuming the company is a viable operation, the retiree needs only minimal interest in the fund itself, how it is invested, or how it yields the pension money. While the pension payout belongs to the retiree, the underlying fund does not. This approach is called a *defined-benefit plan* because the benefit is defined by the factors of years of service, average salary, and the ratios developed in the plan.

A *defined-contribution plan*, like ours, establishes the amount the retiree receives on the basis of three factors:

1. The amounts which have been contributed by the retiree
2. The amounts contributed by the institution in the name of the retiree
3. Any returns earned (or lost) on those invested funds

Suppose, for example, that a faculty member had contributed 5% of each years' salary throughout her career, and the university had contributed 10% of her annual salary to an account at TIAA-CREF in her name. That money will be invested and may grow. The total amount constitutes the faculty member's retirement savings. The amount the faculty member receives periodically during retirement will be a function of (i.e., *defined by*) the total contributions plus investment returns in that account. Prior to the recent changes, the retirement savings fund had to be accumulated at TIAA-CREF and could only be used upon retirement to purchase an annuity from TIAA-CREF. Therefore the fund typically supported a periodic payment which was actuarially calculated to continue until the retiree's death, at which time all payments ceased (with the possibility of provisions for beneficiaries).

In the case of a defined-contribution program, the retirement savings belong to the participant, and the basic thrust of the recent changes has been to recognize the implications of that fact. Since the fund belongs to us, and since it establishes the level of retirement payment, the investment success of the fund is of vital interest to us. By contrast, the underlying fund of a defined-benefit program belongs to the company's pension fund, and the prospective pensioner does not have to be interested in the management of its investments.

Having described the differences between defined-benefit and defined-contribution programs, we can return to the discussion of the literature on retirement planning in general. Since defined-benefit programs have been dominant, there is not much treatment of defined-contribution programs in general literature. In the business world, there is a form of defined-contribution retirement programming identified with its number in the IRS code: 401(k). However, 401(k) programs are typically treated as supplementary to, not replacements for, defined-benefit programs. In addition, 401(k) provisions are not the same as the provisions of the code which affect our retirement: 403(b) and 403(b)(7).

In a sense, the lack of attention to defined-contribution programs in the general literature is not surprising. In spite of the enormous resources involved and the large number of members in TIAA-CREF plans alone, the choices for those participants were so limited until the recent changes that retirement *planning* was a misnomer. Thus, while there is a body of literature on general retirement planning, it does not address issues of direct concern to us. Finally, while the literature may be largely objective and expert, by its very nature it cannot be individualized.

Financial Planners

The discussion of financial planners has been left until the final section of this chapter in part because recent events cause it to be treated separately and in part because with proper precautions, financial planners may provide advice which meets the three desired criteria: that it be objective, expert, and individualized. Financial planning, as an occupational designation, is not very old. In the late 1970s, five brokerage houses commissioned the former Stanford Research Institute (SRI) to do a study of the prospects for a financial planning industry. Their study was optimistic. The conceptual foundation of financial planning is clear enough: people are inundated with the need to make many financial decisions which may have a substantial impact on them in the future. Those decisions involve, for example, calculating taxes, purchasing a home, buying insurance (life, health, casualty, etc.), paying for the education of children, making investment decisions, providing for retirement, preparing wills, understanding estate and death taxes, and disposing of assets after death. The entire area has become complex in part because significant changes regularly occur in laws, policies, and practices. It makes a great deal of sense to coordinate all these areas of one's life. Enter financial planners.

Presumably, financial planners would know about all these areas and should be able to help develop a coordinated plan which would bring the pieces together into a coherent whole and which would allow people whose professional interests lie in other areas to devote their attention to those areas. Physicians, lawyers, business executives, and academics would probably like to spend the bulk of their working time concentrating on the professional worlds they know well. A financial planner could help arrange and organize their personal fiscal affairs. As an extension of the principle of the division of labor, this made eminently good sense as long as a way could be found to pay for it which would satisfy both those who delivered and those who received the services. Two different approaches developed almost immediately.

Commission-Based Financial Planners

Financial planners might provide planning advice and receive reimbursement by way of commissions derived from financial products they persuaded their customers to purchase. Many former life insurance agents, stockbrokers, and mutual fund salespeople renamed themselves *financial planners* and basically provided their previous sales services with the appearance of financial planning. Customers had the impression they were getting the services of a financial planner without having to pay for them. This apparent discovery of a frictionless financial machine was merely an illusion. The commission-based plans typically suggested that customers purchase financial products which yielded commissions for the planner.

You may want to take advantage of these services. However, you should be aware of the potential conflict of interest. Before you start any sustained conversations with a financial planner, I think you should make it clear that you will want written, complete and full disclosure in the form of an itemized accounting of the commissions the planner receives on each financial product. If the planner balks, scepticism is warranted.

Fee-Only Financial Planners

Some financial planners decided to work only for a fee. They would not accept any commissions. They might help clients implement their plans, but they would not accept any commission—above the table or below—and in many cases they suggested ways of acquiring equivalent financial products free of commissions. These people wanted to be financial planners whose primary interest was the client's (because if they failed, the client would go elsewhere). Their model was that of physicians, lawyers, and accountants, whose codes of ethics make the honest ones among them scrupulous about keeping perceived and real conflicts of interest out of their professional lives. In the more complicated cases, financial planners work closely with lawyers and accountants in developing a complete and coherent plan for their clients. For example, unless such planners happen to be lawyers, they should not presume to draw up a client's will, but they should insure that the will is consistent with the client's total financial objectives and plans. The financial planner could help the client suggest to the lawyer whatever changes might be advisable as the client's financial condition changed. The situation is analogous to the way in which many people use their doctor of internal medicine for their periodic examinations and for reference to specialists as appropriate. While financial planning is not as complicated as medicine, it can be sufficiently complicated that a generalist may not know enough.

The basis of the fees for fee-only financial planners has varied. Perhaps the most popular is that used by lawyers and accountants: billable hours. Others use a percentage of the client's net worth. Some charge a flat fee. One ingenious person who specializes in financial planning for sole owners of small businesses agrees to be paid annually whatever the owner pays the lowest-paid full-time employee. The consistent effort is to arrive at a fee which is *not* a function of commissions or churning accounts but related to the planner's effort on behalf of the client.

As the financial planning industry has developed over the past decade, the distinctions between commission-based financial planners and fee-only financial planners seem to have been purposely blurred by the commission-based planners. I think they would like the appearance of freedom from any conflict of interest which the fee-only planners have, but they do not want to give up the lucrative commissions of the commission-based approach. Thus, some have developed systems in which they do the planning part for a fee, but they receive commissions when they implement the plan. While the vocabulary is not consistent, those planners seem to have developed a new euphemism: *fee-based* financial planners. Perhaps they believe that sounds close enough to *fee-only* financial planners to gain their credibility while retaining the commissions. Once again, I would recommend considerable caution. Other commission-based planners have developed deals with firms such as brokerages whereby the planners pretend they do fee-only planning alone, but in fact they split the commissions with someone else.

We should expect continuing efforts to confuse these distinctions. I think commission-based and fee-based financial planners are wolves in sheep's clothing. They are, plain and simple, salespeople with a new title. For my own purposes, I do not mind dealing with salespeople directly. I do, however, dislike having them try to fool me.

If you consider using a financial planner of whatever designation, the following procedures seem advisable.

1. From the beginning, make it clear that you are going to insist upon itemized full disclosure in writing not only of the payments to the planner but also to the firm and any associated persons or firms. After an early meeting, you might put that request in writing in a letter to the planner, and you might say you will not pay any bills until you receive the itemization.
2. If a planner seems to be trying to persuade you to purchase a particular product or a limited range of products, be suspicious. There are few cases in the financial services world where there are no essentially equivalent products, and you have a right to be told of the equivalent products.
3. Read the documentation for products and discover whether they pay commissions. If they do, insist on being told in writing where those commissions go.
4. Unless you have the utmost confidence in the planner, do not sign or agree to any procedure which allows the planner to trade in your account without your permission.

I think the Securities and Exchange Commission has let the public down on this score. I believe it should establish some designation such as "Professional Financial Planner," which would stand for people who can demonstrate an absence of any conflict of interest, as lawyers, accountants, and physicians can. I believe, further, that the SEC should then monitor the use of that designation. However, the SEC seems to be more a captive of the financial services industry than concerned with consumer confidence. In the meantime, the cautions suggested should give you some protection. The financial planners who will be upset by your request for full disclosure are probably just those you should avoid.

While our annual salaries probably do not justify continuous fee-only financial planning, the importance of our retirement savings does justify a periodic careful analysis by an expert who will objectively pay attention to particular individual circumstances. On the assumption that we can do some of the basic work ourselves, this book suggests in general a two-tier strategy.

First, we might become our own primary financial planners. This book addresses retirement planning on that basis. I have not considered other financial planning issues, such as children's education, support for parents, and so forth, because that is not common to all of us. However, retirement planning is a need we all have. Where other issues enter into individuals' lives, they will need to be considered, and I hope the general approach of this book will help in that process, too. If you become your own primary financial planner, you will be able to meet at least two of the criteria outlined for good advice: that it be objective and individualized. That leaves only the criterion of expertise, and here is where the second tier enters.

I suggest that at important junctures, you consider reviewing your retirement plans with a fee-only financial planner. In essence, the fee-only planner would be giving you a second opinion about the plans you have developed. Using the rough time lines developed earlier, you might consider consultations once a decade. That might mean four or five consultations, though that could be varied more or less depending upon particular circumstances and your willingness to be more or less connected to the development and implementation of your plans. If this book achieves its purpose, it will help you become your own primary financial planner, and it will help reduce payments to fee-only financial planners by allowing them to concentrate in their area of expertise.

If you find this suggested process connects you more to this activity than you would like in view of other more important activities, you might use a fee-only financial planner to draw up plans and go to another fee-only financial planner to get a second opinion. Obviously, that will cost more, but there is a price for those who are not do-it-yourselfers here as elsewhere.

Campus-Based Study Groups

Since people at an individual college or university will have issues of common interest in regard to retirement, it is natural to think of forming campus-based study groups. In encouraging the formation of such groups, I can almost hear a collective sigh concluding with, "Not another committee?!" Having spent twenty years in academic administration, I employed one of the tricks we like to use: I did *not* refer to a committee. (However, the effect is the same.) I know many of us feel that our campuses have been committeed into stasis, and I know many of us feel that committees spend most of their time on the contemporary equivalent of discussing how many angels can fit on the head of a pin (i.e., what is the largest number of students we can cram into a course and still call it a *seminar*). I think it was Parkinson who said the function of most committees is to keep minutes and waste hours. Nevertheless, this suggestion *is* different. (Isn't that what all administrators say?)

I suggest that people with common interests could agree to meet periodically to discuss the issues raised as a result of the changes in retirement. Some of these issues commend themselves to investigation by a few people who would share their efforts with others. Throughout the book, you will see topics on which further information is needed. There is no need for each faculty member to investigate each topic alone. It would make more sense to share the results of our investigative efforts. The needs and interests will overlap considerably, and since the groups would be campus-based, the conditions will be common among different members. Conversations can then be focused and relevant. (Compare *that* with the last committee meeting you attended.)

In addition, such study groups would not need to come to any politically contrived conclusions. (Compare *that* with any committee.) Neither this book nor a study group can dissolve your responsibilities for making your own decisions in regard to your own special conditions. The most you will be able to acquire is additional information that might be useful as you prepare to discuss your own plans with a fee-only financial planner.

Another advantage of a study group would be to share information about prospective financial planners. Not only would members of the study group be able to visit and assess prospects, but also I am reasonably sure that financial planners would be willing to address such study groups to discuss issues and make their services known. In addition, of course, as TIAA-CREF develops its LIFE stages program, study groups would be a natural source of invitations.

Part Two

Early Phases

3

Early Career and
Early Preretirement Planning

Introduction

It may seem strange to suggest that you begin thinking about retirement when your career is just starting; however, that is one of the consequences of a defined-contribution retirement program. Prospective retirement savings will start to accumulate early in your career, and their treatment may make a great deal of difference in later years. Suppose, for example, that a twenty-seven-year-old person has a $30,000 salary from which she contributes 5% and the university contributes 10%. If that $4,500 is invested so that on average over the next forty years it earns 7% more than inflation, and if she retires at age sixty-seven, that $4,500 will be worth over $72,000 in uninflated dollars. If, however, the $4,500 were invested so as to just cover the impact of inflation, it would be worth $4,500 in uninflated dollars at the time of retirement. Obviously, that will make a considerable difference in the quality of her retirement. Thus, there are important decisions to be made, and it is worth considering them from the start.

However, we should not exaggerate the effective range of decisions and the importance of making the right ones at this stage. In the early years of your career, there are more important decisions to be made, and the funds which start to accumulate are not of sufficient magnitude to warrant excessive attention or concern.

Paying Off Student Loans

If you are typical, you will have left graduate school with a substantial backlog of loans which must be paid off eventually. Some of those loans may be government-based. Some may be commercial loans cosigned by friends or relatives. Still others may have been made directly by family members or friends. The best financial advice I can give you is to get rid of that debt burden as soon as you can. In a sense, it is unfortunate that some of the lending sources, such as families, may be patient with the return of the principal, because this can breed a false sense of security where there should be little. In general, as we move along in our careers and personal lives, our commitments grow larger and our salaries, unlike those of our colleagues in other professions, will not grow so much that later income might make such indebtedness appear trivial. In general, it would be wise for you to discharge the debts and get your personal balance sheets into a positive net worth condition as soon as possible.

Managing Your Career: Tenure

It is difficult for me as a faculty member and former academic administrator to discuss new faculty careers without commenting on the attainment of tenure. For twenty years, I played a central role in making tenure decisions in regard to scores of faculty. The negative ones were almost always painful, and the positive ones were rarely easy. It is tempting to launch into a disquisition on the history and practice of tenure, but this is not the place. The social purpose of tenure is to protect academic freedom so that students will have an education undiluted by faculty looking over their shoulders, and so that research can be conducted without concern for transient popularity. Tenure has achieved that social goal. However, the price has not been paid by the society at large which benefits from tenure but by faculty members themselves through reduced mobility and consequent lower compensation.

In order to help you achieve tenure so that planning for retirement is something more than an empty exercise, I would like to give a few words of advice. Almost all tenure decisions turn on three areas of consideration: teaching, scholarship, and service. Different institutions may emphasize one area rather than another. No matter what you may be told—even in writing—you will be well advised to present as strong a case as you can in all areas. I think you should be suspicious of those who tell you that you can get by if you turn in a lackluster record in any area. You should also be suspicious of those who say they can politically manipulate your attainment of tenure. There is no doubt that faculty with lackluster records have made it through the tenure grid, and there is no doubt that some campus politicians have manipulated the system for others. However, the tenure review process is growing more sophisticated each year, and in the best institutions, it is already quite sophisticated, involving careful review processes and faculty peer review committees. In the old days, perhaps it was easier to fool administrators and to manipulate them politically. However, successful faculty know what is reasonable to expect, and it is difficult to manipulate a committee composed of accomplished people who already have tenure. If you wish to achieve tenure, I think you should present the best case possible in all areas.

TIAA-CREF Participation

In many institutions, you will be brought onto the TIAA-CREF system immediately. Some institutions have a waiting period, and the next section suggests actions to be taken in the face of that institutional penuriousness. In some cases, there may be room for maneuverability, and you may feel so strapped for cash that you are tempted to take advantage of the flexibility by not joining until it is unavoidable. In general, that is unwise. If the university makes contributions to retirement plans, you will forgo receiving that money and any compounding growth from its investment. While retirement may seem an eternity away, your older colleagues can tell you that eternity passes more quickly than you imagine. In my years of talking to academics about their retirement, I have not met any who wish they put aside less in the earlier years. Thus, I would suggest that you join as soon as possible.

IRAs and SRAs

Individual Retirement Accounts (IRAs) and Supplemental Retirement Annuities (SRAs) have two features which they also share with your regular 403(b) retirement plan. First, money is put into them on a tax-deferred basis. That means the money is subtracted from your gross income, which lowers the amount on which you pay income taxes. Consequently, your income taxes are lower in the year in which you make a contribution to an IRA or SRA. Second, investment gains in your IRA or SRA accounts, like those in your standard 403(b) account, are not subject to income tax in the year in which they are earned. Do not become too excited. This is not paradise. When you finally take money out of your IRA, SRA, or 403(b), you must pay income taxes on all the money you take (since you have not paid it previously).

The positive features of this tax-advantaged situation are supposed to be two-fold:

1. There is a presumption that your income taxes will be lower in your retirement than they were prior to your retirement. That is a particularly difficult presumption to validate; my sense is that tax levels are more a function of politics than economics, and political events are even more unpredictable than economic events.
2. The growth from investments occurs in a tax-free environment, which means it is not eroded by annual taxes. This feature seems to be positive and proven.

IRAs differ from SRAs in that the former are established by you personally, and the latter are established through your institution with the help of its benefits offices. Briefly put, I think the best device for establishing an IRA is through mutual funds (see the appendix), which usually provide you with help and appropriate forms. Be aware of charges for maintaining accounts. They can destroy any gains you might make. At this stage, I would suggest using TIAA-CREF or any other financial organization with which your university may have close contacts to establish your SRA. You do need to assess your eligibility for deductible IRAs or SRAs, and of course you need to determine if you can afford to defer the income (apart from deferring income taxes). Under current regulations, if you need to take out any money before you are fifty-nine and a half, you will not only have to pay taxes, but you will also be assessed a 10% penalty by the IRS.

In 1981, tax legislation was constructed so as to allow any person to establish an IRA and to contribute $2,000 to it in before-tax dollars. In 1986, the regulations were changed to be considerably more restrictive. By and large, IRAs went out of the lexicon of many financial planners when their clients were already in a pension plan. The general reason is that the post-1986 regulations state that people covered by "approved" retirement programs are not eligible for before-tax IRAs. A TIAA-CREF plan is such an approved plan.

However, an exception was granted for people who are covered by an approved plan but nonetheless poorly paid, and you may fit into this class. In general, in 1991, if what is called your Adjusted Gross Income (AGI) is less than $25,000, you *may* be eligible to have a before-tax IRA. The regulations are somewhat complicated, and some of the eligibility criteria depend upon whether you have a spouse, the level of his or her AGI, and how you and your spouse file your federal taxes. If the combined income of you and your jointly filing spouse is less than $40,000, you *may* be eligible. Take special note of the fact that the issue relates to your adjusted gross income (AGI), which is a technical term. You can easily determine your AGI for any year in which you have paid federal income taxes by looking at the line which designates AGI on the return. You will note that it is lower than your total income.

You may create an IRA "backwards." It is not necessary to create the IRA by the end of the calendar year to which it is applied; you may create it at any time before your tax return is due the next year. After you receive your W-2 forms and have other accounting of income and expenses, you may calculate your AGI for the previous year by filling out your appropriate 1040 form (which you have to do anyhow). If you find that your AGI for the previous calendar year is less than $25,000, you may create your IRA and recalculate your taxes, which will be lower if that is the only change you make.

Even if your adjusted AGI is greater than $25,000, you may be able to create a partially funded before-tax IRA. The rough numbers are as follows: for each $1,000 you make over $25,000, subtract $200 from the maximum before-tax IRA you can create. At $35,000 for the single filer and $50,000 for joint filers, the benefit is phased out entirely. There are academics who have an AGI of less than $35,000 alone or $50,000 jointly. They are eligible for a full or partial IRA, and it would be wise to investigate the possibility carefully. The IRS has materials and regulations; you can fill out the forms to determine eligibility.

As this material is being prepared, politicians are debating whether the restrictions on IRAs should be relaxed or even returned to the 1981 conditions. It will be smart to watch those developments and take advantage of them if you can afford to do so.

There is another condition in which you might consider an IRA. Some institutions have delay policies for participation in their retirement plans. If you are a new appointee in such a university, you might consider establishing an IRA for the period in which you are not covered. Of course, the better procedure is to negotiate full participation immediately upon appointment, especially since the institution is recruiting you. However, universities are not immune to the bureaucratic rigidities of other organizations, and the people who are actively recruiting you may not have the flexibility to grant an exception. In my experience, typically, the university administration has the ability to grant exceptions, even though it may say initially that the re-

strictions are part of the contract between the university and
TIAA-CREF.

There are three provisions for IRAs worth noting and repeat-
ing.

1. Currently, taking a distribution from an IRA before age
   fifty-nine and a half is accompanied by a 10% penalty unless you can meet rigid criteria of need, such as disability.
   Again, there is some discussion about relaxing this provision, and you will need current and accurate information
   before taking action.
2. When you withdraw money after age fifty-nine and a half,
   income taxes will be due on the entire amount received
   (principal and earnings) since they have never been paid.
3. IRAs may be *rolled over* from one account to another. If,
   for example, you are dissatisfied with the mutual fund you
   selected originally, you may find another and move the
   money from the first account to the second. Typically, the
   new account managers will help you with the paperwork
   on that decision. The rollover must be completed within
   sixty days to avoid an IRS declaration that acceptance of a
   distribution has occurred and, thus, the 10% penalty and
   requirement of income tax payments.

These provisions may be discovered with the IRS instructions
and forms, and if you decide to set up an IRA, you should read
the latest instructions carefully.

I suggest that you keep any IRAs strictly separated from
other accounts, especially any after-tax savings. When it is time
to take distributions from your IRA, you do not want the IRS
to declare that your after-tax savings should be subject to the
taxing provisions of IRAs. That would amount to double taxation on your money. The easiest way to prevent any confusion
is to be sure the accounts are clearly separated.

SRAs were another form of retirement savings which were
widely available previously. Basically, one could set aside up
to 20% of income in an SRA. Those were pretax dollars which

also accumulated in a tax-free environment. Initially, they were accessible without penalty for a broad range of needs before retirement—for example, for children's education, housing needs, medical needs, or other educational purposes. Once again, the regulations changed. The age limits of withdrawal for IRAs were imposed on SRAs, and more severe restrictions as to participation were instituted.

The current contribution limits for people in TIAA-CREF plans work as follows. The regulations for your regular retirement program indicate that before-tax annual contributions to TIAA-CREF by you and the university should not exceed $9,500 or 20% of your income, whichever is less. (Twenty percent of $47,500 is $9,500, and since many universities have adopted a pattern of contributing 10% to TIAA-CREF while requiring the participant to contribute 5%, it may be useful to know that 15% of $63,333.33 is $9,500.) Thus, faculty members in a TIAA-CREF program at the cumulative 15% level *may* be eligible for an SRA if they are earning less than $63,333.33. In the enabling legislation, there is no provision for adjusting the $9,500 for inflation.

If you are a participant through TIAA-CREF or through another approved plan, the organization will usually be willing to help you set up your SRA. It is probably best to fund your SRA through a payroll deduction. If you want to transfer your SRA funds elsewhere in the future, you can do so relatively easily (assuming your university does not try to constrain you).

Finally, you may be eligible for both an IRA and an SRA. Suppose, for example, your AGI were $25,000 and you and your university were taking less than 20% of your earnings as a contribution to your TIAA-CREF program. If you could spare the cash flow, you might be able to select both. I do recognize the catch-22 aspect of what I am saying. While you may be eligible, you may not be able to afford to defer the income. That is why I said earlier that IRAs have largely gone out of the lexicon of financial planners. I suspect the legislators understood the dilemma also, and that is why they were willing to grant the exceptions.

Property Ownership and Wills

As retirement comes closer and personal relationships become more complex, the issue of wills becomes more important. People who do not have a valid will are said to have died *intestate*. However, there is a sense in which everyone has a will. States have what are called *probate procedures* for disbursing assets after death. The probate process either follows the directions of a valid will or, in the absence of a valid will, it has established rules and procedures. Intestate probate may be expensive if there are any complications or disputes. In addition, it may end up distributing assets in ways the dead person would not have wished. Suppose, for example, that a faculty member has been living with a companion to whom he wants to leave his property if he dies unexpectedly. There might be a car, a book collection, furniture, pets, and so on. Unless some provision is made, the state will *not* designate or allow the distribution as the faculty member wishes. Under intestate probate procedures, the property will go to members of the dead person's family. Only if those family members accept the distribution and then give it back to the companion will the process end as the dead faculty member wished. In the previous sentence there is an important word: "Only if those family members *accept* the distribution." People are not required to accept whatever is distributed from a will. They have the right to refuse. If they do so, the property goes to the next person in the line of succession by designation of the probate process. Thus, a prospective recipient might unknowingly refuse a distribution intending that such refusal would make the property go to the companion. However, it will not go to the companion; it will go to the next in the line of succession. That person might not know anything about or care anything about the former companion.

Even if the faculty member and companion were married, absent a will or some other provisions, the faculty member's wishes that everything go to the spouse would not be fulfilled. In most states, only half the property automatically goes to the spouse; the other half goes to the rest of the family (e.g., the parents). A will would avoid all these complications. However, you should not assume that you can draw up a valid will. There is something of a movement designed to help people draw up wills without the help of a lawyer. Nevertheless, there are enough technicalities and special provisions in state laws that I think that is a questionable procedure. The less complicated the situation, the lower the attorney's fees; the more complicated the situation, the more important a carefully drawn will is. However, you may feel that in view of the value of your property, paying an attorney is not warranted.

An alternative procedure exists which has appealed to people with uncomplicated lives and is sometimes referred to as the *poor person's will*. The procedure simply establishes the direction of passage by virtue of ownership of property. If, for example, property is jointly owned, then it passes irrespective of a will or intestate probate processes. Ownership rights supersede provisions of a will. Thus, as long as all your concerns relate to identifiable property which can be designated with regard to ownership, you may be able to create the conditions you desire by means of ownership designation. There are four forms of ownership to consider.

1. Individual Ownership. In this situation, you own the property outright. There is no joint participation. Upon your death, the property will pass through the probate process and be distributed either in accordance with your will or in accordance with that state's intestate procedures.
2. Joint Ownership, Tenants in Common. This form of ownership does not have to be between married people. In this form of ownership, you may do whatever you wish with your interest in the property. The owners have an undivided interest in the property, and they are responsible for a proportionate share of the expenses and income from the property. You might dispose of your share as you see fit. You may sell your share, give it to someone else, or dispose of it through your will. You cannot do anything in your will which affects the share you do not own. Upon your death,

under this form of joint ownership, your share will be distributed by the succession process designated by probate either as specified in a will or as designated by the intestate process.

3. Joint Ownership with Rights of Survivorship. This form of joint ownership does not require that the owners be married. The interest of each of the owners passes automatically to the other owners upon the death of one. In this form, your interest will pass automatically to the other owner(s) upon your death. Thus, if four people owned something jointly with rights of survivorship, and if one of them should die, then three people would jointly own the property automatically. This condition supersedes anything written in a will. For example, suppose four people own something jointly with rights of survivorship, but the person who dies directed in her will that her share should go to a fifth person. That provision of her will would not be honored, and the three would automatically own the property. If all four should die in rapid succession, then the entire property would be disposed of as indicated in the will of the last person to die.

4. Joint Ownership, Tenants by the Entirety. This form of ownership can occur *only* between legally married people. It operates like joint ownership with right of survivorship in that upon the death of one spouse, the entire ownership passes automatically to the surviving spouse, and it takes precedence over any provisions in a will. Suppose, for example, a married couple held property jointly as tenants by the entirety, but the husband really did not want his wife to have the property after he died, and, without telling his wife, he put a provision in his will assigning his interest to someone else. That provision of his will would not be honored. An advantage of this form of ownership, where appropriate, is that only 50% of the value of property so owned is included in the estate of the first spouse to die, and the cost basis is advantageous.

In short, many of the conditions of a will can be accomplished by paying careful attention to forms of ownership. That is not recommended where the circumstances are complicated or where nonproperty interests such as guardianship of children are important. In the context of retirement savings, it is, of course, very important to designate beneficiaries with care. Such designations, also, supersede any provisions of a will.

Allocation of Retirement Savings Accumulations

Some universities offer some choice about whether the retirement savings funds are invested through TIAA-CREF or through some other corporation. It is difficult to recommend that a junior faculty member or administrator spend much time or energy investigating such alternatives. There is no evidence that you or I can pick investments or other funds which will yield better results than can be achieved through TIAA-CREF, and the amounts will be small enough that the issues of diversification, which become important as the retirement savings increase, do not loom large at this stage. Given the level of funds involved at this stage in your career, the general track record of CREF and TIAA probably give you enough security.

Previously, TIAA was a fixed-income fund, and CREF was an equity fund. Thus, the only way faculty members could invest a portion of their investment cautiously was to put it into TIAA. That is no longer true. CREF now has a so-called Bond Market Account which, while it does not duplicate TIAA's investments, serves the function of a fixed-income fund. A disadvantage of the CREF Bond Market Account is that it is new and thus does not have a well-established track record.

Correspondingly, there are two disadvantages with TIAA. First, TIAA has so far refused to itemize the current values of all its investments, which means that its investment success or failure cannot be subjected to the scrutiny of the general professional financial community. Thus an investment in TIAA must be done with more than the usual blind faith. You may ask how you might know whether the CREF Bond Account is better than TIAA as an investment medium, and the answer is—literally—you cannot know. Since TIAA will not tell you precisely what it is doing, you will not be able to make a comparison between it and the CREF Bond Account or, indeed, any other fund, whether part of TIAA-CREF or not.[1] Second, TIAA has operated according to a provision that if you wish to withdraw your (non-SRA) funds from TIAA, you may do so only over a ten-year period under rigid rules. On balance, my concerns with TIAA's policies lead me to suggest that if your choice for fixed-income funds is confined to CREF's Bond Account and TIAA, you should choose the former. Presumably your career is not entirely settled at this stage, and if you were to move to a place which did not do business with TIAA, you might find a ten-year withdrawal policy frustrating. I have no evidence that your money will be safer or will earn more in TIAA than the CREF Bond Account, and if your money were in the latter, at least you would be able to judge its performance relative to competitors.

While TIAA-CREF has removed some of the constraints which it previously placed on the use, allocation, and distribution of retirement funds, the new opportunities will be made available only if your college or university allows you to use them. As of the writing of this book, a significant proportion of the institutions have not elected to grant these opportunities to their faculty. Their reasons are even more difficult to fathom than the reasons that TIAA-CREF resisted the changes in the first place. At least one could understand why the executives of TIAA-CREF had little interest in giving up their monopoly. However, the university gains nothing by maintaining the restrictions. As the British might say, they seem to like to take their paternalism neat. Nevertheless, I recommend that while you are in the early stages of your career, you should not spend much time or political capital attempting to get your university authorities to change. You have too much of importance to concentrate on without getting involved at this point in your career. The impact on your lives will not be all that dramatic yet.

Even if your university has made no changes as a result of the recent developments, there will be decisions for you to make as to allocation. Before the recent changes, one of the few decisions faculty members could make about the investment of their retirement savings concerned the allocation of new contributions to TIAA versus CREF. Even then, there were only five possibilities: (1) 100% to TIAA, (2) 100% to CREF, (3) 75% to TIAA, 25% to CREF, (4) 50% to each, (5) 25% to TIAA, 75% to CREF. Now, even within TIAA-CREF, the situation is more flexible.

Prior to March of 1990, the question which I was asked most frequently by people who were still far from retirement was how they should exercise the limited options given them by TIAA-CREF for the allocations of their funds. The rules of TIAA-CREF made the decision difficult. However, any money which was transferred out of CREF into TIAA had to stay in TIAA and could not be transferred back into CREF. There is more flexibility now, even if you leave all your savings in TIAA-CREF.

The earlier basic distinction between TIAA and CREF conforms to a general distinction in investment opportunities between investments which emphasize safety of principal and fixed income on the one hand, and investments which emphasize potential for growth in principal and keeping up with the impact of inflation on the other hand. TIAA, the CREF Money Market Account, and the CREF Bond Market Account represent the former; the CREF Stock Account represents the latter. The Social Choice Account is a mixture of the two.

For the purposes of the analysis here, let us assume your funds are divided between a fixed-income orientation and an equity/growth orientation. There is a trade-off between safety from loss of principal on the one hand and protection against inflation on the other hand. It is a trade-off because no one has yet found or created the perfect investment which does both. What ration, then, should you personally use for your investments?

Some people believe that they can predict the future of the

economy and the future of the investment markets. I am not among them, and I do not know of anyone who has been able to do so over a sustained period. If you believe you can make such predictions successfully, and if you are willing to bet your retirement future on your prognostication skills, then the best strategy for you to follow is to invest heavily in the equity/growth side when you believe the financial markets are in a period of growth by putting 100% of your funds in the CREF Stock Account. When you believe the period of growth has run its course, and the financial markets are going into a period of stagnation or decline, you should move 100% of your funds into the fixed-income side, such as TIAA, the CREF Bond Market Account, or the CREF Money Market Account, depending upon when you believe the next turn will come. If you are really good at these predictions, you might consider being a consultant to some of the major investment houses for a few hours a week. You will be paid very well, and even though you might continue in academia because of personal interest, you will not need to read the rest of this book because your academic retirement savings will constitute only a small portion of your wealth.

However, since the evidence is convincing that no one has yet been able to predict consistently and accurately the direction of the financial markets, I shall turn to answering the question posed without the benefit of prognostication. The primary issue driving the decision should be your age, not your guess as to the future of the economy. Let me go to extremes to make my point. Suppose you were advising someone who was in his mid-nineties about how to make the allocation. Your concern for the impact of inflation on that person's life would be quite small. Your primary concern would probably be on assuring that the principal was protected in order to insure adequate income to cover the person's living expenses. Thus, you would lean heavily toward a fixed-income allocation. At the other extreme, suppose you were advising people who wanted to make an investment for their recently born granddaughter. Suppose they told you they wanted the funds to be used for *her* retirement. Your concern for the impact of inflation would be considerable, and you would want to make sure that money grew as much as possible in the meantime. Thus, you would lean heavily toward an equity/growth allocation. This extreme analysis suggests that unless you have some very strong reason to believe you are a better economic prognosticator than others have been, your allocation decision should turn primarily on your age.

For the sake of simplifying this analysis, let us say that as humans we have an effective maximum life span of approximately one hundred years. Some people manage to exceed that number, but they are such a small exception that we can use the generalization. That hundred-year maximum suggests that we might adopt as a rule of thumb that our fixed-income investments should approximate in percentage what our age is in years. At birth, we should be 100% in equities/growth; when we turn one hundred, we should be 100% in fixed income; and at our fiftieth birthday, our retirement savings should be about evenly divided. I would not want to have this suggestion taken as a new case of numerology. There is nothing magic about it, but it makes sense to me as a rough guideline.

In order to acknowledge the imprecise nature of the guideline, I would suggest, in addition, that the percentage should approximate one's age plus or minus ten years. That means that people who are more inclined to take risks in the hope of better payoffs might be at one extreme of the range and people who find themselves staying awake at night because they believe their retirement savings are in too risky a position might adjust the proportion. It also means that my suggestion for a ratio can carry someone to 110 years of age. Anyone who makes it that far should call me for further advice—I want the advice.

Since we are involved in issues with regard to your age and your retirement, you should consider all the funds on which your retirement will depend—your SRAs, IRAs, your funds in TIAA-CREF, and so on—before you examine the ratio. I am not suggesting that you readjust your retirement savings each birthday. People who find that their actual ratio differs by more than plus or minus ten might want to ask themselves why they have decided to deviate. There may be good reasons for doing so, and if there are, it makes no sense to stay stubbornly with this rule of thumb.

Leaving a TIAA-CREF Institution

Under the new procedures, if you terminate employment with your TIAA-CREF sponsoring institution, you may have the right to withdraw your funds from TIAA-CREF. As indicated, TIAA still retains the right to force you to withdraw such funds in approximately even amounts over a ten-year period. Withdrawal might be considered especially useful if you intend to leave all TIAA-CREF employment entirely. However, remember that some universities require a year's delay for newly appointed faculty to join the TIAA-CREF pension program if they are not members of TIAA-CREF when hired. Thus, if you should withdraw entirely, you may be at a disadvantage when you return to another university position.

Before the recent changes, when participants in TIAA-CREF left TIAA-CREF institutions, they had to leave their money in TIAA-CREF and could only get it out by dying or through an annuity offered by TIAA-CREF when they retired. That has changed, and one suspects that other TIAA-CREF procedures will loosen up even more over time, though there is no guarantee, and there is always the danger that TIAA-CREF will try to reverse the gains made, and *your* money will be tied up again.

However, if you are convinced that you are leaving institutions which can use 403(b) provisions completely, you may wish to consider withdrawing your money from TIAA-CREF entirely. There are potential tax implications to such withdrawal unless within sixty days you roll the money over into an IRA, so you should have the destiny of your funds established before you actually begin the withdrawal.

4

Middle Career and Middle Preretirement Planning

Introduction

As we move along in our careers, important changes usually take place in our professional and personal lives. Our retirement savings begin to accumulate and become significant. Further decisions need to be made about the investment of those funds and funds which will be added to them. Suppose, for example, that in the first decade, someone's salary had averaged $37,750. Using, for example, a 10% rate of contribution by the university and a 5% rate of contribution by participants to their retirement savings and a reasonable rate of return on investment, the retirement savings entering the second decade of service might approximate $100,000. At that point, if not before, decisions about distribution and diversification should be given more serious consideration. Matters of this nature change gradually, and it is not sensible to suggest absolute crossing points. However, some changes may warrant different decisions. In addition to changes of this nature in the retirement savings, there are often changes in our personal lives. We may establish more permanent relationships, start families, and find that our parents have become more dependent on us for support and help. Finally, while retirement may still seem distant, further steps in preparation for retirement are warranted. At this stage, you have much more flexibility than you are likely to have later. It is a time to begin preliminary examination of how the retirement phase of life will shape up, so that you can make adjustments where necessary.

Examine Institutional Restrictions

In the previous chapter, I suggested that while you are in the early stages of your career, you might avoid involving yourself in the political processes which may be required to change institutional arrangements for retirement, especially those made by virtue of a contract with TIAA-CREF. I suggest just the opposite at this time.

You should determine what is permissible in your university, and, if you have been at a number of institutions, you should determine what those institutions have decided to permit. The constraints of previous institutions are currently interpreted by TIAA-CREF to hold even for people who are no longer at those institutions. It is clear that I am not sympathetic with the continuing paternalizers, some of whom, unfortunately, serve on committees reviewing these matters to advise the university. If it takes time to change the approach on your own campus, you can imagine how long it will take for you to influence a campus you have left. My suggestion is that if some of your past or present institutions still refuse to allow you to make decisions for yourself, you should encourage them to do so as soon as possible. The longer the institution waits, the more limited your choices will be.

Perhaps I have given you some arguments to use when discussing the topic with various people. I believe that you should express genuine appreciation for their concern with your long-term welfare and add that, in the end, only *you* can decide what that actually is. You might add that even though you may make mistakes in determining your interests, surely they can make such mistakes, also. Since, by definition, they do not know about your personal plans and personal situation, they are not in a position to make intelligent judgments about your welfare.

Sometimes I find that the most persuasive arguments with authorities are legalistic ones. I suspect there may be an opportunity for legal action here, since the university authorities are in effect constraining your use of your money. If it could be shown later that you would have done better with your money absent their constraints, you might have room for action against them. The important thing to establish in *everyone's* mind is that it is *your* money. Once TIAA-CREF makes an alternative available, in my view, the university is in a very weak position to prevent you from exercising options over your money.

In addition, I would recommend supporting those people who wish to encourage TIAA-CREF to remove the remaining restrictions which it imposes on its participants. I think the goal should be to accept the flexibility which is allowed in the law. This is a time in your career when you are in a particularly good position to suggest these changes. I presume you are part of the tenured faculty or established staff, and yet you are far enough from retirement that you can advocate change without becoming anxious because of your own personal situation. You can advocate the appropriate changes in TIAA-CREF also. If historical precedents are a reliable guide, TIAA-CREF will yield only reluctantly, and it will not always proceed even in its own best interests.[1] Even though the recent changes have been radical, many changes remain to be made in the universities and in TIAA-CREF. This is a time in your career when you are in a position to be an effective advocate for those changes.

Diversification and Administration of Accumulations

The emphasis in this section is on the question of the diversification of funds beyond TIAA-CREF to other investment managers. Following the comments of the previous section, I should point out that, as of the writing of this chapter, something less than 50% of the TIAA-CREF participating institutions permit investments outside TIAA-CREF, and even there, the permitted flexibility is often quite limited. For example, many of the institutions which permit investment beyond TIAA-CREF have concluded arrangements with only a few other investment companies, so where there is some flexibility, it may be severely constrained.

Under the new changes, in the early accumulation years, TIAA-CREF operates like a mutual fund from the faculty member's perspective. It accumulates and invests the contributions in the faculty member's account, and it attempts to make those investments grow in accordance with the objectives of the funds in which the faculty member has placed them. In writing annuities, TIAA-CREF functions like an insurance company, and that function is relevant near the time of your retirement. At this stage, your primary interest is in its mutual fund function and alternatives to that.

General Explanation of Mutual Funds

It will be most useful to concentrate here on what are called *open-end* mutual funds. They are so named because they allow new shareholders to enter as they desire. The funds offer to sell a limitless number of new shares. New shares are bought from the fund itself, not from someone who already owns shares (as is typical of stocks), and when owners wish to sell their shares, they sell them back to the mutual fund; they do not have to find someone to buy them.

A mutual fund may own a variety of financial instruments (e.g., stocks and bonds). The management of the fund makes investment decisions on its behalf. There are two distinct advantages to purchasing mutual funds: the first is proven, the second is widely advertised but not as convincingly proven.

The first advantage is that a fund provides diversification which an investor would not otherwise be able to obtain. For example, consider a $2,000 IRA. To go to the extreme for the purpose of illustration, suppose you used all your IRA money to purchase stock in one company. The value would then rise and fall with the price of that particular stock. While you might have considerable opportunity for gain, you would also have considerable risk because, to use a favorite metaphor of the trade, all your eggs would be in one basket. Mutual funds are a way to use the same $2,000 and achieve investment across many different corporations. Diversification diminishes the risk considerably. By combining the investments of many people, the fund is able to invest in a broader array of companies than the individual could invest in alone. The mutual fund can invest in the broad range of stocks which individual investors might like to have invested in, but could not because they did not have enough capital to diversify as a mutual fund can by combining the investments of many people. By investing the $2,000 in a mutual fund, the investor gets a fractional interest in a number of stocks, and thus automatically achieves diversification.

The second advertised advantage to a mutual fund is that investors gain access to professional managers who are good at predicting the future of the financial markets and therefore at making money for their customers. It is an interesting theory which has a problem with reality: there is no solid proof that it works. For example, there is an index, Standard and Poor's 500 stock index, which is a computer-based tracking of five hundred stocks. Presumably because of its breadth, it represents general market movement. It is a purely mechanical representation of the market. One might think that with the application of intelligence, professional managers could beat the averages. One would think so, but it just is not true. Some managers do seem to have more success than others, especially over short runs, but some people have more success at games of chance than others over the short run, too. Probability theory says that must be true.

There is no evidence I know that professional managers can beat the averages. In fact, collectively, they tend to fall behind the averages (probably because no one has to pay the averages to be average!). *The Wall Street Journal* recently created an amusing exercise which pits successful, highly paid, and presumably the "best" investment managers, which it calls The Pros, against a selection of stocks it dubs the Darts because it is selected by employees throwing darts at the stock market page. As this material was being written, some results of the exercise were reported. Even in these circumstances, seemingly rigged to favor the Pros, the Wall Street Journal reports as follows:

> In a series of 15 six-month contests, the pros and the darts are almost even. The professionals have won eight times, and the Dartboard Portfolio has won seven times. Considering that it costs nothing to throw darts at the stock listings, while professional investment advice can cost quite a bit, those results don't speak too well for the pros.[2]

In recognition of the failures of professional money managers to beat the averages, some mutual funds are purposefully designed to *match* the averages. They are called *index funds*. The managers of those funds do not try to beat the market; they try to imitate the behavior of the averages as closely as possible. They use computer programs to accomplish their task, which is, after all, one which ideally could be carried out by a machine.

Thus, the primary reason for selecting investment through a mutual fund is to gain diversification. If diversification through a mutual fund is good at a low level of total investment, then at a high level of total investment, it must also be good to seek diversity among mutual funds. Thus, one might want to put investments in a variety of mutual funds and thereby achieve even greater diversification, safety, and reduced volatility.

In describing the concept of index funds, the operations of the CREF Stock Account are included, since it is basically an indexed fund which attempts to imitate Standard and Poor's 500 index. Another aspect of the CREF Stock Account makes indexing advisable. To put the matter nonquantitatively, CREF is an enormous fund; it may be the largest equity fund in the world. As such, it has a financial version of the potential for being muscle-bound.

Although the number of shares issued by a major corporation may be quite large, only a relatively small proportion of them trades on any given day. If the CREF Stock Account were a managed fund instead of an indexed fund and if the CREF managers were to decide one day that a particular stock in the account was overpriced and should be sold, the very volume of CREF's sale would probably depress the price of the stock. It would probably not be possible to sell all CREF's holdings in the stock at what the managers thought was an overrated value. Similarly, if the CREF managers thought some stock was underpriced and issued purchase orders, their very activity would probably drive the price up, and they could not acquire much of it at what they thought was an attractive price. If, however, they decided to sell or purchase only smaller amounts, the impact on the total portfolio might be so small that it would not accomplish the desired result (assuming they could predict the market accurately over the long run). In short, CREF's problem is the obverse of ours as individuals. We are too small to matter, so we invest in mutual funds; they are so big that everything they do which is significant to the fund matters to the market at large. The strategy for handling this problem is to act through indexing.[3]

Now, perhaps, the reasons for my general suggestion that in the early stages of your career you might leave the growth-oriented portion of your retirement savings in the CREF Stock Account are more clear, at least from an investment-management perspective. The CREF Stock Account is designed to imitate the economy in general, and if you have faith in the viability of the economy and believe that the stock market will beat inflation over the long run, the CREF Stock Account is a reasonable place to put your funds as they begin to accumulate.

At the middle stage of your career, however, your accumulation may have reached a more significant level, and a reasonable question arises about a new layer of diversification: diversification among mutual funds. Clearly, it would be foolish to put all one's money in one stock or bond (unless one had solid insider knowledge); thus, it is almost surely better to have money in the CREF account than in a single instrument.

And while one could argue that it is better to invest in a fund that imitates the market than in one with substantial risk, it is equally persuasive to argue that some diversification of investment managers or computer programs is wise (especially since no index fund yet created has been able even to keep up with the indexes over a sustained period of time). Almost surely, if a *fee-only* financial planner interviewed someone whose retirement savings were all in one investment management organization, the financial planner would suggest some diversification. In thinking about this issue or discussing it with others, you should not be distracted by attempts at a *reductio ad absurdum* argument which would drag the recommendation to ridiculous extremes. I am not suggesting that you should invest in a large number of mutual funds. However, at some level of asset accumulation, more than one mutual fund or one management organization seems prudent.

The following rule seems sensible: Do not keep more than $100,000 or 20% of your funds, whichever is greater, with one investment manager. That means that you do not need to begin diversification until your retirement savings reach $100,000, and it means that if you have $1 million in retirement savings, you would have approximately $200,000 with each of five investment managers. I think it is unlikely that many academics will reach or exceed $1 million, but those who do should probably increase the number of investment managers by one for each $200,000 unit. Having different funds will also give you a good window on the activities of a variety of funds, their services, their responsiveness to questions, and their performance. If you intend to leave some funds with TIAA-CREF, this would mean that you might be looking at three or four more fund managers. In my view, that is not an extraordinary amount of work.

Some people are so far toward the disconnected end of the spectrum that I discussed earlier that they will want to avoid even this level of personal involvement. I recommend against such a strategy, because I think it assumes too high a risk. However, if you are willing to accept the risk in order to be disconnected, it would make sense to stay with CREF, since they have been involved with academics for many years and remaining with them will require the least effort.

The appendix describes mutual funds in much more detail and suggests a means for choosing among them. If you think some diversification would be prudent and you are in a university which permits such diversification, you might want to read that appendix as a preface for action or to prepare for meeting with a fee-only financial planner.

Wills

At this stage in your career, if you have not done so already, you should consider the preparation of a will. Whether or not the "poor person's will" mentioned earlier has been sufficient, your life and commitments have probably changed enough that you should have a will. You may have children, or elderly parents, or other people who are dependent upon you. Mere incidences of ownership will not be sufficient for their care. For example, if you have children, you should make some provision for their care and guardianship. It is even wise to suggest a succession of guardians in case the first guardians either cannot or will not accept responsibility when the actual time comes. Certainly, one should discuss these prospective provisions with the guardians and, where appropriate, with the children.[4]

The creation of a will should involve the designation of an executrix (female) or executor (male) who acts as your representative after your death. She or he must operate within the provisions of your will, but there may be some flexibility. A good executrix or executor can be a valuable source of personal counsel for your family and friends, and she or he may be able to head off the conflicts and controversies which can lead to adversity, broken family relations, and high legal fees.

There are two different forms of executrix or executor which you might choose: another person or an organization. The advantage of the former is that human contact from the right person will be appreciated by those who survive you, especially at a time of grief and unhappiness for them. A smaller advantage is that a personal executrix or executor usually charges less for her or his work; thus, greater resources will go where you wish. An executrix or executor who is also an heir may not charge for services rendered. There are at least three disadvantages of a personal executrix or executor. First, there is a possibility of emotional involvement that would exacerbate any potential conflicts. Second, in general such an executrix or executor is an amateur involved in what could be a complex and technical process. Third, the person designated might die before you do and before you make the appropriate changes in your will, which would mean that you would die without designating an executrix or executor.

The advantages of choosing an organization as executor are objectivity and existence in perpetuity. The disadvantages are impersonality and the fees charged. Banks are a common choice. However, I have known cases in which we had to push and prod a bank to act. By all appearances, they were happy to continue collecting fees and seemed to have little interest in a speedy settlement.

The executrix or executor is legally liable for carrying out the provisions of your will, and you should be sure to provide the appropriate protection and an appropriate fee. My suggestion would be something like a minimum of $2,000 with a maximum of 1% of the value of the total assets which pass under the will (remember, for example, that jointly held property will not pass under the will). You should also provide for sufficient access to funds to pay legal fees and any other fees. Corporate executors are likely to be more expensive; my estimate would be about twice what I have suggested for individuals. No individual should see this as anything but a service for friends. If she or he sees it otherwise, you need a different executrix or executor. Of course, the designation should be discussed with the executrix or executor, as should the provisions of the will and the intentions which go into those provisions. While a will must be executed in accordance with what it says and not in accordance with what someone thinks he or she remembers the deceased intended, it is easier if the executrix or executor knows what was intended. If she or he sees areas which might prove ambiguous, those provisions can be clarified before the will is finally drawn.

It makes sense to discuss the will with a fee-only financial planner because that person may have some worthwhile suggestions. After the issues have been carefully considered and discussed with appropriate people, it is time to talk with a lawyer with the intent of drawing up a formal will that reflects your desires. The lawyer may have suggestions, but if you have done the preliminary work, the lawyer can concentrate on legal issues and not on general personal counseling. That will help keep the legal fees at a more reasonable rate.

Some people say they have no interest in a will because their situation is so simple. Since academics often do not have large estates, some of them fall into this trap all too readily. However, a will is not created to benefit the person who will die; it is designed to benefit those who remain. It is an act of grace and decency to them. As indicated in the previous chapter, if the conditions are really uncomplicated, drawing up a will is easy and inexpensive; if the conditions are complicated, having a will is very important. Since I have been trained as a philosopher, I have a pretty active imagination for thinking up what we call counterexamples, but it is hard for me to imagine any counterexamples to the proposition that people at this stage in their personal and professional lives should have a will.

Determining Present Financial Worth

One of the actions which will make drawing up a will easier is determining your current financial condition. That determination is also important as you begin to think about preparations for retirement. While some general financial planning books make this exercise appear complicated, determining your financial condition is not difficult, especially if you remember that the purpose is only to gain a general understanding of your financial worth.

You can start by listing all your assets in dollar values. First, you might list the accumulations in your retirement funds, your other investments, your IRAs, your savings, any cash you keep in your checking account, and so on. To that you might add the net value of your house (after subtracting any mortgage), and include other tangible assets with real or significant value. The purpose is not to prove your success as a prospective accountant, so there is no need to go to extremes, and you may decide not to include some items even though they may have marketable value. I never include the value of my automobiles because I experience automobiles as a relentless liability, though I recognize they have some monetary value. I do not include family heirlooms, items of significant sentimental value, or the family pets. Even though all have some marketable value, the circumstances under which I would sell them are so extreme that their value is not worth calculating. For example, I have a few books which I inherited from my grandfather who taught mathematics and physics in the first part of the twentieth century. The books discuss ether as if its existence is unquestionable! Some people have told me some of those books might be valuable on the rare book market. However, I do not know how valuable they are, and I cannot think of any circumstances in which I would sell them, so I do not include them in my calculation of my assets. My general rule is to include those items I would be prepared to sell if I needed extra money. Once you have completed that exercise, you have some sense of your total assets.

Next, you should develop a list of liabilities stated in dollar values. Included in that list should be continuing charge account balances, loans on cars, student loans still outstanding, other outstanding loans, and so on. Be sure to account for any house mortgage unless you have accepted the procedure suggested above of stating your house value net of the outstanding mortgage.

The dollar assets less the dollar liabilities will yield your approximate net worth. If it is negative, you have some work to do to find ways of saving. The greater your net worth, the more prepared you are for large expenditures, whether unexpected, such as major repairs to a house or a new car, or expected, such as children's education and your retirement.

Some people find it useful to prepare approximate statements of their projected net worth for the years ahead as they prepare for major passages in life, including retirement. That is a useful aid in financial planning for retirement.

Some people also find it useful to take an accounting of their cash flow situation. It is possible to have a positive net worth and to still be strapped for cash. Retirement accumulations, for example, may create an attractive net worth, but since in general they are not usable during working years, they will not help pay immediate bills. People who come up short regularly in terms of cash flow are probably draining their net worth and may be setting themselves up for substantial problems later.

I think it is best to do this exercise in approximations and in round numbers—you may be able to sustain your interest that way long enough to get it done. If you waste time trying to chase down every dollar and, perhaps, arguing with your partner about it, you can miss the forest for the trees. The task is to arrive at a reasonable approximation of net worth and of your cash situation, so that you have some sense of your actual financial security and your ability to meet financial obligations.

If you are a parent, sometime in this period or later you may find yourself faced with extraordinary educational expenses for your children. It seems that colleges and universities are re-examining and withdrawing their previous commitments to help pay the tuition of children of faculty and academic staff. (It has seemed a bit more than ironic to me that the frequent explanation for this change in heart is that rising tuitions have made the "benefit" too expensive. Did the children cause tuitions to rise so dramatically?) If you face a need for substantial funds for these purposes and others, you may find it useful to know that as of October, 1991, you may borrow against any SRAs at TIAA-CREF. The interest rates are approximately equivalent to corporate bond rates, which are likely to be better than you can do on your own. There are numerous restrictions imposed by TIAA-CREF and some imposed by the IRS, but the alternative may interest you. If you do borrow in such a manner, be sure to subtract that obligation from your net worth.

Estimating Retirement Needs

It is not too early at this stage to think about retirement needs. Retirement may still seem distant, but if, after doing the projective analyses and estimating your needs, you find that you may not have enough money to carry you through retirement, you still have time at this stage in your career to take some action (including changing your career if necessary). If you wait too long, it will be too late, and you will have to live with—and suffer through—the consequences. Again, at this stage, we are considering approximations. Precision is not necessary; in fact, it can be dysfunctional because it can induce a false sense of complacency (or fear).

In considering retirement needs, we have to enter into a debate which has not been resolved. Many retirement advisers have suggested that income after retirement can be safely calculated at some fraction of the needs of income before retirement. Their arguments go as follows: the retiree no longer needs to make some purchases (e.g., clothes, luncheons in restaurants, etc.) which were perhaps necessary while employed. In addition, many retirees have their houses paid for, so that mortgage payments do not reduce their income. Some advisers argue that retirees should make new, more economical housing arrangements, such as moving into a smaller house or an apartment. Some suggest that the retiree should go from owning two cars to owning one. The list of savings which the advisers project goes on as far as their imagination allows (though most of those doing the imagining are not themselves retired). In the matter of creating and funding retirement plans (which is the source of most of this reduced-income argument), it is naturally in the interest of the funding agency to argue for reduced needs, because that will justify reduced payments to the actuarially constructed defined-benefit fund or reduced contributions for our plans.

However, if the question is one of imagination alone, it is not difficult to imagine that, while some expenses will decrease, others will increase. Medical expenses are the most obvious, though many other items may also be needed to make an aging person's life more comfortable. In addition, at least in the early years of retirement, retirees may incur other expenses (e.g., travel which has been put off). The advantages of an employment situation will no longer be present, and duplicating them may create some expenses. If the exercise is merely one of imagination, it would seem that two imaginative people could argue to a trade-off in regard to needs immediately before and immediately after retirement.

I think some unexamined assumptions continue to linger in the world of general retirement planning. For example, there seems to be an assumption that the retiree is the only person in the family on a payroll and that retirement for him (*sic*) means a changed life-style for everyone. However, the family before *his* retirement has probably depended upon *his* income, and it will probably continue to depend upon it. Thus, real living circumstances should be taken into account as the needs are calculated.

In addition, it seems reasonable to suggest that retirement needs as a proportion of preretirement earnings change with the level of income: the poorer people are before retirement, the more likely they are to need the same income in retirement. By contrast, the wealthier people are before retirement, the less they may need to approximate their preretirement income. Take the matter of housing as an example. The person who is barely able to afford adequate housing before retirement probably needs similar housing after retirement. In addition, the poor person was probably in rented housing, so the only way to reduce expenses is to move to even smaller rental space.

However, the wealthy person may have had housing which is far more than adequate after retirement and may be able to save considerably by "downsizing." The wealthy person may have owned the house(s), and may be able to gain usable retirement capital by selling property. I believe this is an important perspective because, while we as academics are not properly classified as poor, we are generally not wealthy either. Thus, we are likely to require an income that is near the level of our preretirement income.

Another assumption which the general retirement planning literature appears to make is that the retiree should be prepared to make some quite dramatic changes upon retirement. Those changes include not only living at the new lower retirement income level but also moving immediately to new housing, often perhaps relocating, changing life-style expectations, and so on. At least in this book, that is deemed generally inadvisable. Retiring is a substantial enough change without causing all sorts of other changes. In the longer run, retirees may wish to make those changes, and they may even be forced to do so, but if it is avoidable, it would be sensible not to make all of those changes immediately upon retirement.

Finally, much retirement planning seems to be based upon an assumption that retirement is a relatively short period of time before death, and that the period of time can be treated as a single homogeneous unit. That is unlikely. In the first place, retirement is typically a lengthy period of time. It is not unlike starting a new career and is likely to last for another twenty years or so. During that twenty years, there will be substantial changes in the life of the retiree. The person will perhaps start as an active and vigorous person ready to do many things which previous employment conditions prevented. In general, during the retirement period, the aging process is likely to become more obvious and to restrict a person's activities. Thus, although people may need approximately the same level of income immediately upon retirement, they are likely to need significantly less as time goes on. Since much of this depends on individual circumstances, it is impossible to indicate who will go through what processes on what time schedule. However, current retirement planning, whether through pensions or annuities, presumes that upon retirement, everyone needs some fraction of the preretirement income and that the level of need will remain constant throughout retirement.

My suggestion is that in general, immediately upon retirement, you will need approximately the same income you had just before retirement. Then, we might reasonably suggest that those needs will decline in constant dollars, so that by the time of your death, they will be some fraction of your needs immediately upon retirement.

Let us carry the analysis further and add more precision, recognizing that you may have good personal reasons for changing the parameters of the analysis. Many retirement specialists suggest that the amount of annual retirement income needed approximates between two-thirds and one-half the exiting compensation (in constant dollars) and that a steady constant-dollar income level throughout retirement will be required. I suggest it makes more sense to assume that you will need more in the early years than in the later years. Thus, I suggest that, as a generalization, you should start with approximately 100% of the exiting salary.

As a result of the previous analyses, I use a more generous estimate of *average* income needs during the retirement years. I suggest three-fourths of the exiting salary (in constant dollars). We might, then, set up a declining constant-dollar table of need, so that immediately upon retirement you need 100%, and toward the end of retirement, you need 50% of the exiting salary in constant dollars. Rather than a straight line, it makes sense to visualize it as a gradual downward curve in the early years, followed by a sharp decline in the middle years, followed by a leveling off in the late years, so that by the end of the life expectancy of the retiree, the income in constant dollars levels off at about 50% of the exiting salary. The graph in figure 4.1 depicts this suggestion by year, so that it can be used to project annual needs. Appropriate calculations can then be made to determine how to plan total retirement funds to achieve the

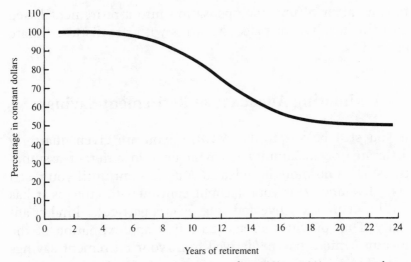

Figure 4.1. Annual retirement income needs. 100% to 50%; average of 75%.

goal. This analysis is discussed later, after we introduce some other factors.

This graph is presented only to indicate how the analysis might be performed. The parameters of the graph might be changed, with a consequent impact on the retirement planning to be analyzed. For example, people whose homes are entirely paid for and whose universities supply medical benefits in retirement would have lower net needs. The personal variations are substantial, and it may be that no two people will have the same graph. However, an analysis such as this should enable you to start developing an estimate of your retirement income needs.

I have purposely kept this analysis in a different section from an analysis of how much will be available. Many retirement planning suggestions, even those offered by TIAA-CREF, seem to assume implicitly that the faculty member needs only what will be available. That may not be true, and later I suggest, some strategies for dealing with situations in which what you project to be available will not match your needs. Obviously, however, need is somewhat related to availability. You cannot turn a career of undercompensation into a retirement based on affluence, but the place to start is with a realistic estimate of need.

Estimating Adequacy of Retirement Savings

If you still belong to TIAA-CREF, you are given quarterly estimates of an annuity payment on two different assumptions: (1) if no more is added to your account until you reach sixty-five and (2) if your account continues to grow as it has until you are sixty-five and you select a particular kind of annuity. That provides an adequate first approximation of the income which may be derived from your retirement savings with TIAA-CREF, and you can use it in conjunction with an estimate of social security savings, as discussed below.

If you have invested some of your savings in places other than TIAA-CREF, you can make some reasonable assumptions about the growth of your accumulations there and use some reasonable assumptions about what they might earn in retirement to estimate the retirement income they might provide. Suppose, for example, future contributions for you are made to funds other than TIAA-CREF at the rate of 15% of your annual salary. You know your current salary, and you can estimate its growth over the years until, for example, you reach sixty-five. Each of those salary estimates will yield 15% to add to your retirement savings account. Make some assumption about the success of the investment program (for example, 10% annually) and some assumption about the impact of inflation (for example, 4% annually). Those estimates should yield an estimated retirement savings fund. Using that, you might assume some income level net of inflation from those savings (for example, 6%). You then have an *estimate* of the income you will have from both your TIAA-CREF funds and your own managed savings funds. Your next task is to estimate the payments you will receive from Social Security during your retirement.

Estimating Social Security Payments

There are three different ways to make this estimate. First, you can use the formulae which the Social Security Office uses, and you can estimate your coverage and credited service. In the end, you will arrive at some number which, again, should be good enough for the purposes of this exercise. Second, you can get a copy of the appropriate tables from a Social Security office, estimate your coverage and credited service, and use the tables to make an estimate.

Third, you can adopt my suggestion and save yourself some arithmetical work. If you go to any Social Security Office, you should be able to get Social Security Form SSA-7004-PC-OPI titled: "Social Security Administration Request for Earnings and Benefit Estimate Statement." You will see that it is a simple form to complete. You should fill it out and send it to:

Social Security Administration
Wilkes-Barre Data Operations Center
P. O. Box 20
Wilkes-Barre, Pennsylvania, 18703.

If you cannot find the appropriate form, you may write to the same address, or telephone. The Social Security Administration maintains a toll-free number for requesting the form: 1-800-234-5722.

About six weeks after you send in the completed form, you should receive an accounting of the earnings credited to you. In addition, you should receive an estimate of your future social security benefits, depending upon how you have filled out the questions as to retirement date, and so on. If you want to examine some alternatives, for example with regard to dates of retirement, send in another form (they will accept photocopies). They do not respond creatively to multiple requests on a single form or multiple requests in a single envelope.

When you receive the estimates, you should also receive the Social Security Administration's accounting of your participation in Social Security—the crediting for past employment. It is wise to check this information, also, in case there is a discrepancy between what you think should have been credited and what they have listed. Beyond reducing the amount of arithmetical work, the listing of your credits is one advantage that the suggested procedure has over doing your own estimating. If you believe there is an error in the crediting by Social Security for your account, you can look back over your records if you have retained them. If you have not retained them, you should be able to get help from university personnel department(s) to verify what your coverage has been. If you have kept your past tax forms, another source of information is the year-end W-2 forms.

New legislation was adopted some years ago which started a system of what is called *wage indexing* with regard to social security. Under the new procedure, it is no longer sufficient that you be covered for forty quarters; you must also achieve certain minimal levels of earnings (and, therefore, contributions to Social Security) to have full coverage. The minimal levels with which the new system started have increased rapidly (about 7% per year compounded), so that they now have an impact on salary levels of faculty members and administrators. For example, in 1990, you will have to have earned $51,300 per year to have a full year of coverage. Obviously, some faculty approaching retirement will not have been paid at that level in 1990 and will not receive full coverage for that year. That means they may not receive the maximum social security payment when they start to receive their checks. If you have worked on a reduced compensation basis in a given year, you may not have had the full coverage credited to your account, and you will not receive the maximum social security payment. Be sure to check the accuracy of the statements sent to you.

Beyond your university-based retirement income and social security, you may want to take into account income from other sources of savings. For example, you may have inherited a significant amount. I would make three points. Be sure when you are deciding how to invest such sums that you take the nature of the investments (fixed versus growth) into account when you make your total allocation decisions. Second, you can use the process suggested for 403(b) savings retained in accounts outside TIAA-CREF to estimate the income which might flow from those savings. Third, in so far as possible, I suggest that you use such money first to supply your retirement income. In that way, you will leave the retirement savings working in the tax-free environment longer, and you will have a tax advantage for your early retirement income.

In regard to any inheritance you think you may receive, I suggest considerable caution. Such intentions have a way of being miscommunicated and of being changed unpredictably. In addition, while the actuarial tables for expected deaths are reasonably accurate, individual persons have a way of defying them. In general, in personal matters especially, I suggest treating such distributions as unexpected pleasant additions to one's life-style rather than planning on them. One additional positive aspect of treating them as unexpected additions is that one is less inclined to engage in those postdeath inheritance fights which can tear families and friends apart and reimburse lawyers handsomely. However, there may be cases in which the probability of receiving a substantial inheritance is so great and the amount is so significant that it would make a difference in basic living (for example, a decision to retire early or extend a sabbatical leave).

One should also include in this calculation of extra income royalties from publications, sales of personal art works, and expected consulting fees, though in the latter case, especially, wisdom suggests caution. Once out of the appropriate networks, many faculty and administrators find their services are not so readily sought. As to royalties, scholars sometimes find their scholarly materials become dated even in immutable areas such as philosophy. Again, there are exceptions, and it is foolish to ignore those exceptions in constructing a plan, but there is wisdom in suggesting caution.

As you make these estimates, you should also consider

anyone else's retirement income, such as that of a spouse, which will have a significant impact on your retirement. I have already indicated that I can do nothing more than suggest that you pay attention to this prospect. The number of possibilities is so great that it would be impossible to say anything useful without knowing details. However, if the income from such sources is potentially significant, then you certainly want to consider it.

These estimates are for a first approximation only. They will help you estimate at this stage whether your retirement savings will be adequate. This form of estimating does not suggest how you should actually handle your retirement savings. That will be discussed later, and as you approach retirement, you will be able to—and should—make more accurate estimates. The total prospective income should be able to deliver something approximating your estimated preretirement income at the time of retirement. If it is not, now is the time to take corrective actions. The next chapter presents alternative strategies.

Significant Changes in Retirement Arrangements

In the past few years, there has been some movement toward making significant changes in retirement plans for faculty members and academic staff—for example, moving the retirement plan from a defined-contribution plan to a defined-benefit plan or vice versa.

In general, I believe that defined-contribution programs are to be preferred over defined-benefit programs. Both plans are equally susceptible to paternalistic treatment, so there is no substantial difference in that regard. However, the funds for the defined-benefit programs actually remain with the employing organization or its designee, so there is a stronger argument that it is their fund to do with as they wish consistent with the law. The primary difference which recommends defined-contribution programs to me is that they are much less subject to behind-the-scenes manipulation.

One of the principal political reasons for ERISA legislation arose out of defined-benefit programs which were presumed to be funded out of the current income of a corporation. The presumption was secure enough until the corporation went out of business, at which point the pensioners became merely one group among a number of creditors seeking some small portion of what they had been promised as a pension. In short, many people were simply out of luck and had to fall back on social security as their sole means of support. ERISA legislation changed that situation in regard to the corporate sector, so that such defined-benefit programs had to be funded in accordance with appropriate actuarial principles and reasonably conservative investment assumptions. However, even in the corporate sector, it would be wrong to think utopia has arrived in the matter of funding for defined-benefit programs. First, within ERISA legislation, there is considerable flexibility. Second, the agency's monitoring staff had been underfunded for nearly a decade. Third, some corporate executives retain actuaries, accountants, and lawyers who are, as it is said, "creative" in responding to the constraints of the legislation as they determine the amounts which must be supplied to fund the program or the amount by which the program might be overfunded. You can imagine how eager some executives would be to retain your firm if you could show that the retirement fund had been overfunded and that resources could be returned from the fund to the company to show a more attractive bottom line.

Defined-benefit programs, from before ERISA to the present, are subject to considerable manipulation. My concern is that the money will not be there when it is time for you to receive your pension. Recognize, also, that since defined-benefit programs pay their pensions based on longevity and recent salaries, that formula can be changed. In fact, it is sometimes changed in order to encourage early retirement, which strains the pension funds to produce the pensions. In early 1992, the Bush administration proposed legislation which would put additional pressure on employers with defined-benefit programs to fund them adequately. The intensive lobbying effort that employers have mounted to defeat that legislation cannot be comforting to employees supposedly covered by the plans.

The points just made need to be emphasized even more strenuously in regard to defined-benefit programs which are funded through state government agencies. Public defined-benefit programs are attractive sources of funds for politicians. In addition, they present an opportunity to pay off political favors by legislating pension concessions. That means that they provide opportunities to make short-term political gains with early retirement programs which win popularity contests by reducing state employment in the short term but leave the bills to a longer term when the politicians will be beyond reach. My observations suggest that the capacity for manipulation and deception is limited only by the moral conscience of the manipulators. Of course, there is a long-term problem: at some point the fund will not be able to support its liabilities in terms of pensions. What then? The quick answer is that since the pensions will be an obligation of the state, the state will *have* to pay them. (Which is why the politicians want their piece of the action, too.) However, what if the voters refuse to pass the bond issues or budgets which would support these obligations? There will be a mess, and time will drag on, and the lawyers will get rich. Presumably the federal courts will order the payments, but people may not have received their pension payments. What if the court order drives the state into bankruptcy? No one knows, and I, for one would rather find out as a result of watching disinterestedly than as a result of having my retirement funds sequestered.

Finally, I do not really think people should be indifferent to investment policies, even in defined-benefit programs. If I were a state employee in a defined-benefit program, I would not be comforted to learn that the managers of some state funds had entered into future contracts. I know such investments *can* be made on a hedge basis and thus may be conservative. However, I would not be comfortable with such "quick buck" schemes. I would be doubly discomforted to discover that the initial forays had been successful—that would only whet their appetite and that of others.

Anyone who is complacent about public or private defined-benefit programs should read the lead article in a recent issue of *Barron's*: "Gnawing on Nest Eggs: Pensions at Risk." The reporter discusses many of the tricks which are used in both the private and public sectors which lead to frightening prospects for these pension funds and to the question whether they will be able to support the pensioners when the time comes. More directly relevant to faculty and academic staff, the reporter interviewed Kenneth Codlin, the investment director for the Illinois State University pension fund:

> The higher education fund can cover about 50% of its obligations, Codlin says. The other Illinois state pension programs are about 60% funded. . . . As for the fund Codlin manages, 'It looks like we'll literally go broke—run out of money altogether by the year 2017—if we average 8% return on investment between now and then. Raise it to 10%, and you could add only a few years. We could stave it off with 20% annual returns, but I don't know where you get them.' "[5]

The article also reports that some years ago the State of Illinois decided not to have its faculty and academic staff participate in Social Security so they will not have even that as a safety net.

By contrast, in defined-contribution programs, once the money is distributed to your account in your name, it is your money, and your future is much more in your control. Thus, if your state is contemplating forcing faculty members and academic staff to move from a defined-contribution program to a defined-benefit program, I suggest that you do what you can to prevent the adoption of the legislation. Unless you mount a major effort, you are not likely to be successful, because the reason the defined-benefit pension fund administrators want you in the fund is that it gains more short-term resources for the fund.

TIAA-CREF has been effective and aggressive about persuading states to adopt alternative funding for faculty and academic staff so that they can make a choice between the state defined-benefit retirement system and TIAA-CREF's defined-contribution system. My suggestion is that unless you are yourself a powerful political figure, you should adopt the defined-contribution system where possible.

We are left, then, to consider a class of people who may have been forced into the state retirement system after they had accumulated a significant amount of TIAA-CREF savings. What should they do? If they are likely to seek employment in a TIAA-CREF participating institution in the near future, they might wish to keep an account open at TIAA-CREF just because of the possible waiting period mentioned earlier. If not, it is difficult to find any grounds for recommending that they leave their funds in TIAA-CREF. Certainly, I think it would make sense to begin the ten-year-process of withdrawing from TIAA.

Part Three

Preparations for Retirement

5

Late Career and
Intensive Preretirement Planning

Introduction

As retirement comes closer, you should become more directly involved in your own retirement planning. This chapter assumes you will have a broad range of alternatives available. If you intend to withdraw your funds from TIAA, remember under current TIAA rules, that is a ten-year process; thus, you will need to consider taking that action in this period, or the issue may become moot. If your current or previous universities continue to forbid you to gain access to your own retirement savings within the constraints of law, you will have to make the appropriate adjustments as you read the chapter.

For some years, there will be a special class of people who will need to make additional adjustments: those who are already approaching this stage but have lived within the historical constraints imposed by the previous provisions. They will not be able to do much about foregone opportunities, but the sooner they take advantage of the new opportunities, the more control they will have over their retirement.

Planning Retirement Timing

One of the first issues you now face is the timing of your retirement. That timing is much more in your hands than it was until recently. Assuming the appropriate legislation is passed and signed, if you are a tenured faculty member, you will no longer have to retire in June of the year you reach sixty-five or seventy. You may continue with your teaching and research presumably for as long as you wish or at least until the university is ready to demonstrate that you are not qualified. And well you should. Your years of teaching and research should have brought a level of maturity to both which is advantageous. Furthermore, as the average age of students in universities continues to climb and as the image of a campus dominated by adolescents sowing their wild oats recedes in the face of reality, your age, maturity, wisdom, and judgment should be increasingly valued.

Early Retirement

Recently, it has been popular to offer incentive plans for retirement before sixty-five. Those plans have been largely reactive, as administrators and board members think they have found ways to save money through substituting junior faculty for senior faculty. The latest studies estimate that about one-third of the colleges and universities have formal early-retirement programs.

In regard to salary or one-time grant arrangements alone, there is no way to make responsible general comments. The best rule of thumb may be that if you already intend to retire and you are offered an incentive, you should take it. I liken it to the use of grocery coupons: they make sense to the consumer who was already going to purchase that product. I have seen few early-retirement incentive plans in academia which would justify early retirement on fiscal grounds alone. A basic problem is the nature of our retirement program itself. If we were in defined-benefit programs, the authorities could redefine the conditions by which our pensions are established and thereby make a substantial difference in our retirement pension. However, in our program, the major change which would make a significant financial difference would be increased contributions to our retirement savings accounts. Thus, in order to make a substantial difference in postretirement income, a special university grant to the retirement account would have to be quite large and might well overwhelm any gains the university made from trading in a higher salary for a lower one.

In the end, all you can do rationally in regard to an early retirement proposal is to examine *carefully* whatever is offered. If you are tempted to accept a proposal, this may be a time to involve a fee-only financial planner. If you proceed, you should have something in writing, and you should have that reviewed by *your* attorney. You should resist pressures for quick acceptance. The issue of timing retirement is one of those irreversible decisions: you should make it in accordance with your own timetable and interests. Those who argue that you need to make a decision immediately should be treated like stockbrokers who tell you that you *have* to purchase their stock *du jour* or "you will miss a wonderful opportunity." They should be told that you will discuss the possibilities with your advisers.

Early Retirement and Health Care Provisions

This area should be examined very carefully. In general, if you elect early retirement, you will not be eligible for Medicare until you reach sixty-five. Thus, it is very important that you understand what medical benefits are available until that time, even though Medicare does not solve everything.

In the first instance, if you retire early, you should try to persuade the university to keep you on the regular university medical plan(s). If group provisions do not allow that, you should request that you be covered by the university through some device which gives you adequate protection. As the aging process continues, prospective illnesses are increasingly expensive to cure, and the body is less resistant to invasions. Medical expenses can mount rapidly and undermine an entire retirement plan.

If the university will not provide any medical protection on its own, recent federal legislation, known as COBRA, indicates that you *must* be given the opportunity to continue in the group plan in which you have been. The rate will be set at on an individual basis. That will be expensive, and it will only last either eighteen months or thirty-six months, depending upon specific circumstances. You should take that opportunity unless there is a more attractive alternative.

If the university offers early retirement because it wants to maintain a program of incentives for early retirement, I think the university should pay for your health care at least until you are sixty-five and thus eligible for Medicare. It is legal for the university to make such payments, though they *may* be defined as income to you by the IRS. Whether they are defined as income depends, to some extent, upon how the plan is structured, which is another good reason to discuss all these provisions with a trusted adviser.

A most important reason for making sure you have pursued this topic to a satisfactory resolution is that many medical insurance contracts have a "no preexisting condition" provision. When medical insurance companies initiate coverage on a new policyholder, they often require a waiting period for what *they* define as preexisting conditions which they will not cover. Thus, it is important to be sure your medical insurance does not lapse. Whether contemplating early retirement or not, the rule is the same: be sure you know what your medical insurance plan covers and what it does not cover, and be sure there is no confusion or ambiguity. Once again, it makes sense to ask for a third party to examine the situation for you. While the university's benefits office may be an excellent first place to go, they can make mistakes and leave you with no recourse.

You do not want to examine your medical insurance coverage when you are ill. You need to understand it thoroughly while you are well and can take steps to be sure you have adequate and comprehensive coverage. The potential problems of inadequate coverage are enormous—even to the extent of threatening the financial safety of your retirement.

Phased Retirement

Some of the more progressive colleges and universities have begun developing phased retirement programs for faculty. Since (as far as I know) such programs have been confined to faculty members, this section will address them directly. Thus far, only about 20% of the institutions have phased retirement programs, but a larger number have worked out individualized plans on an *ad hoc* basis. As the market conditions for faculty tighten, there are likely to be more formal plans developed. It is a natural system for allowing faculty members to move gradually into retirement and for allowing the institution to have more flexibility as enrollment patterns change. Given the fact that these faculty have proven themselves, from an educational perspective, phased retirement is educationally a much better way to deal with changes in enrollment patterns than the currently popular approach of exploiting part-time faculty, full-time faculty, *and* students.

A phased retirement program might work as follows. First, the faculty member might go from full time, full compensation to ¾ time, ¾ compensation (trading off, perhaps, retirement fund contributions in return for full medical coverage). Next, the faculty member might go to ⅔ time, ⅔ compensation (with the previous trade-off). From that stage, the faculty member might move to ½ time, ½ compensation (following the same trade-off). From that point, the faculty member might move to ⅓ time, ⅓ salary, with no retirement or medical benefits beyond those supplied to all retirees, and from there to ¼ time, ¼ salary, with no retirement or medical benefits beyond those supplied to all retirees, and finally to adjunct status.

Some institutions have been experimenting with so-called cafeteria benefit programs in which the institution agrees to a maximum dollar limit of benefits for each employee and then allows the employee to choose from a wide range of alternatives staying within the dollar limit. Such programs are increasing in popularity and might be useful in the context of phased retirement.

You might consider an agreement—in writing—that until you elect the ½ time or less option, you retain the right to ask to be returned to full-time status. A multiyear arrangement—in writing—could be developed for the phasing process. If you and the university consider such a process viable, you should be sure to consider tax implications.

You should also be sure to examine the social security implications. Such a plan may affect the definition of full coverage for you, and that in turn may affect your ultimate social security payments. If you have actually retired and are receiving social security, there is currently a substantial penalty for working until you are seventy years old. After seventy, there is no social security penalty for working. Certainly, if you are among those blazing a trail, you would do well to talk with a fee-only financial planner. (Perhaps if you are really a front-runner, and the university finds the prospect of phased retirement in general attractive, it may be willing to subvent some of your expenses for a professional financial planner.) In time, viable systems will probably be developed, so the need for external expert help may diminish.

In any event, before starting a retirement process which involves long-term commitments, it makes sense to have a lawyer review all documentation. If the university administrators have their wits about them, they will seek advice from their counsel; you should do no less. Your counsel should have your unalloyed interests at heart. Just because university counsel has signed off on a specific arrangement and just because university counsel may be a pleasant luncheon companion in the faculty dining room does not mean you should accept university counsel as representing your interests.

Establishing a Retirement Date

The section of chapter 4 on "Estimating Adequacy of Retirement Savings," discusses how to estimate what your retirement savings will provide as income during your retirement. That section notes that you will need to make the estimation more precise as your retirement approaches. Now is the time to do so. The preceding section of chapter 4 provides a means for estimating your financial needs in retirement. The following section discusses alternatives for generating retirement income. All these factors should be coordinated as you prepare to discuss the actual date of your retirement with the appropriate authorities. If, for example, you find that even with a generous early retirement program, none of the methods discussed below enable you to meet your estimated needs, you may want to rethink the date of your retirement. The general point applies well beyond the confines of early retirement to establishing any retirement date, early, normal, or late. The longer you continue to work full time, the more you and your university will contribute to your retirement savings, *and* the less you will need to generate under the methods suggested in the next section. You face three important variables: your needs, your estimated income in retirement, and the retirement date. As you contemplate a specific retirement date, you should attempt to establish the precise consequences of changes in those variables. The best way I know to do that analysis is by what corporate planners call *scenarios:* examine realistic alternatives to find a reasonable fit for you. Perhaps you see now why I wanted to keep your estimation of needs in a different chapter from the estimation of income. While they must be brought together eventually, the common attempt to tailor needs to availability of income has led to unpleasant retirements.

Alternative Means for Generating Retirement Income

Having considered issues related to the timing of your retirement, it is time to discuss issues related to providing an adequate flow of income during your retirement years. I examine a number of different approaches. Each has its advantages and disadvantages, and they are not mutually exclusive. You may find some combination most appropriate, or you may find that a changing combination over the period of your retirement is most appropriate. These alternative approaches are discussed here because it is in the preretirement period that they should be considered carefully. No single approach is appropriate for all or even most faculty members. One of the positive benefits of the changes which have taken place is that you are now able to structure your own retirement program in accordance with what best suits your needs.

Annuities

We consider annuities first, since until recently that was effectively the only available alternative. The concept of an annuity is easy to grasp. The insurance company takes your money—for example, your retirement savings—and in return it contracts to give you a formula-derived amount of money periodically for the remainder of your life.

Originally, the amount of the annuity payment was derived by the insurance company on two bases. First, the company's actuaries estimated your life expectancy as part of a group. Second, the company estimated what might be earned on the money you gave them and how they might pay that to you along with paying back some of your principal, so that at the end of your life expectancy your entire principal would be repaid. To put it a little more simply, if you gave them $100,000 and if your life expectancy were ten years, then each year the company could give you $10,000 from the principal. In addition, the company could give you interest on the declining balance. However, instead of giving you a declining amount of money, the company would estimate the amount of interest on the declining balance that your money would earn over the ten years and then divide that interest into even portions and pay that to you each year.

Suppose, for example, the company estimated it could safely project earning 4% each year. Over the ten years, that would amount to total earnings of approximately $48,000 on the $100,000. Dividing the $48,000 by ten years yields $4,800 annually. Thus, the company would estimate that it could return to you each year $10,000 from your principal and $4,800 from interest. The company might then guarantee you a check for $14,800 at the end of each year. That would be your annual income from that source for the remainder of your life.[1]

The great advantage of this kind of annuity is that you cannot outlive it. As long as the insurance company stays in business, the annual payment to you will continue for the remainder of your life. Thus, one of the great fears of retirement—that you might outlive your income—is considerably moderated with the purchase of an annuity.

However, another great retirement fear arose in the 1970s: that even though you might retain your dollar income, inflation would reduce its purchasing power. Some foresighted people recognized a concern with the corrosive effects of inflation before the 1970s. William Greenough, who was chief executive of TIAA-CREF for over twenty years, was one of those visionaries. Contrary to the conventional wisdom of his time, he persuaded TIAA to start an annuity program which would not be based on fixed-income financial instruments but on equities which might grow in their underlying value. He was successful in 1952. The College Retirement Equities Fund (CREF) was created, and TIAA forevermore became TIAA-CREF.

The concept of the new form of annuity was that the distribution would not be made from interest earned on fixed-income financial instruments, but on earnings gained in dividends and in response to the performance of funds invested in the stock market. The formulae used for determining income reflected not a fixed dollar amount but the extent of participation in the earnings of the fund. Thus, income from what was called a *variable annuity* could vary in accordance with the value of the investment portfolio. It might be higher or lower than the income which would be received from the earlier form, now called a *fixed annuity*. The concept of the variable annuity was that the income would be responsive to inflation. Its supporters presumed that its income would come closer to keeping up with inflation, and they reasoned that if it were to yield lower levels of income, that would reflect the economy at large. If all this sounds terribly theoretical, it is. The empirical evidence is at best inconclusive. Neither the 1970s nor the 1980s were "normal" decades in the investment business, so extrapolating from them to empirical validation of the theory is more theological than scientific.

In considering annuities with TIAA-CREF, it is important to remember that TIAA-CREF is both an investment management organization (like a mutual fund management company) and an insurance company offering annuities. Your allocation of funds in the accumulating years (while your money is being invested, as in a mutual fund) might be quite different from your allocation for retirement years, and your allocation in the early retirement years might be different from that in both mid-retirement and late retirement years. An arrangement which is appropriate for your early sixties may be inappropriate for your mid-eighties.

The insurance company survives on its statistical estimations. If one individual lives twice as long as the life expectancy charts say, some other individual will live only half as long. If an individual dies earlier than the charts indicate, the insurance company keeps the money which has not been distributed in the form of annuities. If an individual dies later than the charts indicate, the insurance company will have to pay the annuity for that person's life. If the numbers are accurate, the insurance company should suffer no risk, and it is doing just what insurance should do: pooling individual risks. Like the operators of gaming tables, the insurance company takes its cut off the top before redistributing the remainder to the annuitants, so it gets its share for operating the company first.

It may be helpful if I am more specific about the decisions we face as we contemplate using annuities. One is a timing decision. Previously, most people covered by TIAA-CREF had to start an annuity immediately upon their retirement, but that is no longer true. You now have the opportunity to cash out of TIAA-CREF and put your money elsewhere until you decide that you want to start an annuity. Holding premium dollar amounts constant, the later an annuity is started, the greater the income derived from it.

Purchasing an annuity is essentially an irreversible decision. If you die after paying only one premium of your life insurance, the company will have to pay off the face value of the policy after having received only that premium. Thus, they hope you live a long time and pay many premiums. It is easy to see, then, why the life insurance company may insist that you submit to a medical examination and provide it with access to your medical records. Annuities work on the opposite bets and assumptions. Since, in an annuity, the insurance company is paying *you* rather than being paid by you, it is betting you will not live as long as the actuarial tables indicate. From its point of view, it would be a stroke of good fortune if you died shortly after signing the annuity contract. The company would have your entire lump sum, and depending on the contract, it might owe your beneficiaries nothing. Thus, the insurance company's earlier interest in your health disappears, and it does not require health examinations for you to take out an annuity.

Since the life insurance company wants you to have a medical examination when you want life insurance, *you* should have one before you decide to purchase an annuity. In addition, you might want to have a very direct conversation with your physician(s) about your chances for longevity. If you come from a family with a history of early deaths from currently incurable causes, and if your physician(s) say that you are likely to inherit their propensity for earlier than normal death, you might want to consider alternatives to annuities. On the other hand, if your family has a history of longevity, and if your physician(s) say they see no reason you should not benefit from that longevity, it might make more sense to bet you can outlive the insurance company's estimates. Thus, a clear-eyed assessment of your chances for a long life is advisable.

Along with the question of your own health, you should investigate several companies which offer annuities. There are good reasons to consider using more than one company for your annuities. It is advisable to stay with stable and secure companies, of which TIAA-CREF is one. However, size is not a sufficient criterion, nor is a fancy office building or slick brochures, though insurance companies would like us to think so. To the great surprise of many knowledgeable people, venerable and highly rated insurance companies have gone under recently. Some analysts believe that the insurance business may be working up to a crisis similar to the savings and loan crisis. Fortunately, there are rating services for insurance companies: Standard & Poor's *S&P's Insurance Book*, Moody's *Moody's Insurance Credit Reports*, and Best's *Best's Insurance Reports*. All three rate the insurance companies. The ratings should be available in a good library. My suggestion is that you should stay away from any companies which do not make it into the top two rating categories. To the credit of TIAA, it has received the highest rating from each organization, so arranging at least part of your annuities with them makes sense.

However, the ratings are not foolproof. For example, a major life and health insurance company in the midwest (Farwest American Assurance), had been given an *A* rating from Best for many years, and it failed before it was rerated. In addition, Mutual Benefit Life Insurance Company was given an *A* rating by Best, and as of the preparation of this chapter, it is essentially in receivership. Diversification is the best way to gain some assurance of safety in this context. TIAA seems to be very secure, but it has not faced serious competition previously, and we do not know how it will be managed when it does. In considering diversification among annuities, the issue is how devastating the effect would be on you if one of the companies should go out of business and you were to lose your income from that source. As a generalization, it might make sense to use an analogy to the rule of thumb I suggested for diversification of investments among mutual funds up to a total of $1 million: no less than 10% and no more than 20% with a single insurance company.

As you consider using annuities, you should also consider what kind of annuities you want. Only the general differences can be outlined here. In the end, you need to look at the alternatives offered by various companies and be sure you get the annuities which do the best job of satisfying your needs. One of the most popular alternatives has been discussed already: choosing between a fixed annuity and a variable annuity. The former is guaranteed in terms of the dollar amount of income, but suffers from inflationary risk; the latter presumably makes up for the inflationary risk, but it may provide a smaller dollar income in a particular year.

A second contrast in annuities has to do with the length of payout. Fixed-period annuities last for a specified period of time and then stop paying; lifetime annuities continue to pay as long as you live. It is difficult to imagine normal circumstances in which a fixed-period annuity makes sense, but there is so much variety in the real world that perhaps they are attractive to some.

Another alternative to consider is whether the annuity will have a guaranteed period of payment, which means, for example, that a ten-year period annuity would continue to pay beneficiaries if the annuitant died before the conclusion of the ten-year period. That is, perhaps, a way to deal with the psychological issue of the annuitant dying shortly after signing the annuity contract. It is also a way to attempt to leave something to heirs, though if that is important to you, annuities in general are probably not advisable.

Still another issue to consider is whether the annuity period is to cover the life of more than one person. If it does, a new issue arises as to whether the payment after the death of the first should continue at the full rate or some proportion (such as two-thirds or one-half). I should note that if a married person elects to have an annuity which covers him or her only, then by law the spouse must sign a document indicating an understanding of the implications. It may seem that a spouse would always be foolish to sign such a document, but that does not necessarily follow. In some cases, it may be advantageous for the annuitant to take the single-life annuity rather than a two-life annuity and use the difference to fund a term life insurance policy owned by the spouse on the life of the annuitant. If the nonannuitant spouse dies first, the annuitant simply stops paying the premiums on the life insurance and saves that expense. If the annuitant dies first, the annuity will stop, but the surviving spouse will then have the money from the life insurance policy with which he or she can make new decisions for continuing income. Depending on the circumstances, there may be some financial advantages to this process. Nevertheless, it does underline, once again, the importance of planning ahead for retirement. If a couple chooses the single annuity and term life insurance, the prospective annuitant should look into the life insurance early in order to be sure an illness does not cause uninsurability or a stepped-up premium.

These basic alternatives give rise to a large number of permutations. Some companies may not offer the same possibilities as others, and the salespersons (retirement advisers, annuity associates, retirement counselors, commission financial planners, etc.) often seem to want to confuse issues rather than clarify them. In addition, one suspects that often *they* do not know about all the implications and alternatives they are offering.

From the perspective of annuity income, in general, the single-life annuity generates the greatest amount of income. Each feature which is added (such as two-life, guaranteed period, etc.) reduces the immediate income stream. The benefits of all annuities may vary from one insurance company to another, and along with the wisdom of diversification, there is considerable wisdom in comparison shopping. While asking for proposals and information from companies is appropriate, use extreme caution in depending upon the advice of sales-people, whether they are on commission or on salary. Independent and objective advice, at least in the form of a second opinion, should be considered. The issues are so important and the consequences are so far-reaching that this is probably a time to have a discussion with a fee-only financial planner.

Independent Investment Managers

In investigating annuities, you may find that the assumptions on which annuities are based lead to returns which are disappointingly low, even though theoretically your principal is paid as part of the return. Given the alternative of cashing out your retirement savings, you may wish to consider using independent investment manager(s). The word *independent* is important because it indicates that the manager is not working on commission.

As with financial planners, there are so-called investment managers who are willing to manage your account at an apparently low rate primarily because they will keep brokerage commissions which are generated in your account when trades are made. That source of commission income presents a temptation to "churn and burn" the account, which means to generate commissions by buying and selling when there is no legitimate economic reason for doing so. For example, one can find a substitute stock for almost any individual stock that is as good, from an investment point of view, as the original. Your nonindependent investment manager can then recommend the substitution (of course, without telling you that they are equivalent from an investment perspective). Unless you keep up with the market, you will not know they are interchangeable, and the manager will collect a commission both on the sale and the purchase. (He will also collect a pat on the back from the boss, who watches sales production carefully.) Obviously, the person who benefits from trading in your account has a conflict of interest in making recommendations for you. This just takes us back to wolves in sheep's clothing.

However, as with fee-only financial planners, there are independent investment managers who derive their income from fees which insure that your interests are the most important to them. It is at least possible that a successful independent investment manager will be able to generate a return equivalent to the return of an annuity while maintaining the basic principal of your funds. There is no way to decide whether this can be done in the abstract; it can only be solved by examining numbers in the context of some assumptions. One advantage to using independent investment manager(s) is that the decision to do so is always reversible. If you found you could not live on the return the management is able to generate, you could purchase an annuity. In addition, if you think one investment manager is not doing well enough, you could turn to another.

Professional investment management of your retirement funds also has the advantage of giving you considerably more flexibility. If you need access to your principal for an emergency, you can have it. Once your savings have gone into an annuity, they no longer belong to you. Of course, if you were to use your principal, you would have to recognize that your future income from your retirement savings would be reduced, but you *might* be willing to pay that price under some set of circumstances.

Independent professional investment managers presumably know about the myriad of opportunities and dangers which exist in the investment world, and they are prepared to manage a portfolio for you which is tailored directly to your needs. You should be in some contact with your manager(s) discussing your needs for income and your concerns with the management of your funds. In my experience, the best professional investment managers are like good physicians. Both like to work with people who are actively interested in what they are doing. When they are truly professional, they are neither arrogant nor defensive. Thus, you can be involved to the extent you wish and expect a positive reception. Of course, one great advantage to independent professional management is that you do not have to be actively involved all the time. If you wish to take a trip during which you will be out of touch, you can leave knowing someone is watching over your funds. That raises a point about arrangements with managers.

You may elect to have a so-called discretionary account or a nondiscretionary account. In the former, the investment manager has the discretion to make decisions without consulting with you before each one. That is useful if you are going to be out of touch or if you simply do not want to be very connected with the management of your investments. From the manager's point of view, it has the advantage that changes can be made as opportunities are identified and they do not have to wait until you give your approval. A nondiscretionary account gives you greater daily control over the investment activities, though, of course, you always have the ultimate control of firing your investment manager (I do not suggested giving them tenure!). It also allows you to prevent an investment which is too risky for you. It has the disadvantage of forcing you to be quite involved in the management of your funds. The only generalization about this issue I can suggest is that if you decide to use a commission-based investment manager, you should *not* have that be a discretionary account.

There are three major disadvantages with independent professional investment management. The first is that it is likely to be more expensive than can be justified on the basis of the size of your account. Fees are usually based on the size and activity of the account. There is often a minimum fee and a sliding scale as the size of the assets increases. The only way to discover whether it will be too expensive is to investigate specific opportunities. Before agreeing to any arrangement, you should estimate the fees on an absolute dollar basis and then take that as a percentage of your assets. That number will tell you by how much the manager will have to beat nonmanaged investing to justify the fee. If it is over 1% or 2%, I doubt whether it is reasonable to expect it to be done. My own investigation into independent investment managers reveals the following: most are not much interested in an account of less than one million dollars, and their charges for accounts below one million dollars are disproportionately high. A normal fee among those I investigated seems to be about 1% of the assets, with a reducing percentage as the asset base becomes larger. However, some care must be taken in examining the fees. At least as far as I could determine, the fee typically does not include charges for brokerage and other direct expenses the manager may incur in regard to your account. My estimation is that unless you have a multimillion dollar account, the expense ratio for independent investment management will rise substantially above the ratios I have suggested as maxima for investing in mutual funds. (See the classification of open-end mutual funds in the appendix, under the heading "Objectives.") A second disadvantage to independent investment management is that it is difficult to assess how the manager is doing, especially if the account is nondiscretionary (since that means some of the investment decisions and timing are consequences of your activity or nonactivity). I know of no evidence which shows that independent investment managers do better or worse than other investment managers, such as those who manage mutual funds.

We are led, then, to the third disadvantage. In accepting responsibility for large funds, like college and university endowments, one popular approach is to give more than one manager similar objectives for a portion of the endowment. In that way, the administration can assess how well the investment managers do, at least relative to each other. However, if your retirement savings fund is already at the minimal size that justifies independent investment management, then splitting it up will raise the fees as a percentage, and you may find the prospect of independent investment management disadvantageous. An allied problem is that the manager not only cannot diversify adequately because of the size of your fund, but also cannot diversify among managers, because that will reduce the size of each fund too much. As a rough rule of thumb, I would suggest that unless you have somewhere in the neighborhood of $3–$5 million, you probably cannot justify independent professional investment management.

Banks once had trust departments, which are now often referred to as *private banking*. They also provide investment management services. However, typical academic retirement funds will not be adequate to gain the attention of the best private bankers and maintain diversification of managements. Some investigation of the fees and so forth may be worthwhile. Some bankers may suggest that you put your funds in the bank's general trust account, which operates very much like a mutual fund and for which the fees may be considerably lower. It is an alternative worth investigating. However, if the administration of your funds proceeds on the same principles as a mutual fund, it is difficult to know why you should not purchase mutual fund shares directly. Putting all your funds in one bank administrator's hands is as questionable as putting them in one insurance company annuity or one mutual fund.

There are some tricks in the investment management business, and you should be aware of them—and alert for new variations. As I said earlier, if you want to consider investment managers, be sure you find ones that are independent and work for a fee, like *professional* financial planners. Investment managers who are rewarded for putting you in specific financial products are likely to decide *a priori* that those products are the best.

Another trick is for someone to pretend that she is an independent investment manager who charges low fees because she will write off some or all fees against "brokerage." What that means is that she has an arrangement with a broker—it might be her broker or she might get a cut on directed business—to give her part of the brokerage fee. If the transactions are large enough, the broker can share brokerage with the investment manager and still come out ahead. However, what this means to you is that there will be the same temptation to churn your account in order to generate more brokerage.

Still another trick is to set up an investment management organization but not really customize the portfolio. In this case, the managers actually treat the investment decisions as if they were managing a mutual fund. They structure a portfolio which is essentially the same for all the clients and then move all clients in and out of the same investments at approximately the same time. There is no real customization, but that is presumably what you are paying for.

Thus, I do not think *in general* that independent professional investment management makes sense for most academics. We return, once again, to the financial cusp on which you will probably find yourself.

Self-Management of Investments

While this section is directed most concretely to the management of investments after retirement, if you have not been able to gain some experience with managing investments before your retirement, in general, I would not suggest that you decide to take up the responsibility upon retirement. The ideal situation would be for you to take increasing control over your investments as your career proceeds, so that in the years before retirement you are increasingly in control. Doing so would not, of course, preclude making explicit decisions to leave a substantial portion of your investments with TIAA-CREF.

In suggesting that you investigate the possibility of managing your own investments, I do not suggest that you should attempt to manage your portfolio by purchasing stocks, bonds, and other financial instruments directly. If you were to do so, you would have to decide which stocks to buy, which to sell, whether to be long or short, whether to hedge positions with puts, calls, straddles, futures, or other options, whether to deal in the bond market with its maturity dates, yields, conversions, and so on.

It may seem that I have been hard on professional managers in suggesting that there is not much evidence that they can regularly outstrip the market. In that context, it is important to take note of what appears to be an asymmetrical property of investment management. While I continue to believe that there is not much evidence the professionals can beat the market, there *is* considerable evidence that amateurs can lose a great deal. The downside risk for amateurs in the business of managing a portfolio by buying stocks, bonds, and so forth is substantial, and the likelihood of upside gain is limited. In addition, if you were to decide to manage your portfolio directly, you would find yourself making these decisions on a daily or even hourly basis and reading reams of material, only a small portion of which will be relevant and the vast bulk of which is prosaic. The process is likely to dominate much of your waking hours and, in all probability, adversely affect your academic commitments. Thus, I do not suggest that most academics attempt to manage their portfolios directly. Mutual funds are an indirect way to achieve the benefits of self-management without forcing you to spend inordinate amounts of time. There are both advantages and disadvantages to the self-management of retirement savings through mutual funds, and it may be helpful to identify some of them.

One advantage is that the investment plan will be flexible and personalized. You will be able to respond to changed personal circumstances. For example, if your health were to deteriorate unexpectedly, that might trigger a revision of your previous plans, including plans for generating income for your retirement. If you were locked into an annuity, there would be no flexibility for making those changes. Second, as pointed out above, you can always go from professional or personal investment management to an annuity program. You cannot go the other way, and the longer you wait to institute an annuity, the larger the payments you will receive. Third, in self-management, you retain much more control over your ability to respond to changed economic, political, and social circumstances. For example, if the tax laws changed, you might want to get rid of the mortgage on your house. You also have much more flexibility to respond appropriately to inflation or other economic conditions. Fourth, by retaining some control over investments and retirement financing, you will be able to treat your retirement years as a period of changes rather than as an unchanging totality. Finally, by retaining control over the destiny of your investments, you will increase the possibility of having something tangible to leave to heirs.

There are also some clearly identifiable disadvantages to managing your own investments. First, if you decide to manage your own investments, you will have to be more connected to your retirement planning, which means that you have not placed yourself on the extreme end of disconnectedness in the spectrum mentioned. That is an especially notable disadvantage also if you have not been allowed to become accustomed to the management of your retirement savings over the years leading up to retirement. A second disadvantage is that you may not be able to earn enough from your retirement savings to provide for the life-style you want to pursue in retirement, and you may start taking too much out of your retirement savings base, thus threatening your future. Obviously, you need to be honest with yourself. If you will be unable to follow a disciplined withdrawal policy, you should think many times before attempting to manage your retirement savings. If you were to use up too much of the corpus of your retirement savings, you would find that even though you can convert into an annuity program at any time, the annuity may not be attractive because the total fund has deteriorated. A third disadvantage is more directly related to some academics who have a propensity to second-guess everyone, including themselves. The simple fact is that in the process of investment management, you will make mistakes. If you cannot suppress whatever tendencies you may have to second-guess, you are likely to drive yourself to distraction and an unhappy retirement.

The concepts behind mutual funds were described in the last chapter. My suggestion is that if you decide to manage your investments, you should do so through mutual funds. I pointed out previously that if some of your funds are in TIAA-CREF, you are already managing those funds through an organization which, for your accumulation years, functions as a mutual fund. Mutual funds in general will give you sufficient opportunities for personalized investment management that there is little need for direct management of a portfolio.

When you wish to pursue the subject of self-management through mutual funds in more depth, you may turn to the appendix. I identify a number of issues which you should face in that process. I present a method for selecting appropriate mutual funds without attempting to forecast either the economy or the financial markets. There are no "get-rich-quick" proposals, because in general I think they only serve to make the proposers rich. I suggest a sensible and careful process which is not shrouded in mystery or claims for special knowledge. As with much of retirement planning, you will find that careful critical thinking is more than adequate.

Retirement Housing

If you currently own your house, it may compete with your retirement savings as your largest asset. It is an asset which can take on the appearances of a liability, especially in retirement, but you can take actions during the preretirement years which will help keep it as an asset and which will give you flexibility and control over your retirement housing. Perhaps the most important decision you will have to make is in regard to the kind of housing you anticipate for the phases of your retirement.

Housing accommodations which may make sense in the early years of retirement may not make sense in the middle or late years. These decisions may have an impact on each other. For example, a decision to retire to a lifetime care community (see chapter 7) will have a substantial impact on your need for living accommodations. In addition, if you decide to continue living in your current house and to receive your primary retirement income from annuities, that may have an impact on what you do about the financial arrangements for your house.

For example, you might consider using some of your retirement savings to eliminate your mortgage before you purchase
the annuity.

There is a tax exemption on the first $125,000 profit real-
ized on the sale of a house. The exemption can be taken only
once; it cannot be used until after you are fifty-five, and once
you use any part of it, you have exhausted the opportunity. If
you have owned a number of houses as primary residences, you
probably rolled over any gain in the houses as you moved from
one to another; that is, you should have filed a form with the
IRS accounting for the changes, but you would not have paid a
tax on gains.

If you are contemplating selling your house and taking advantage of the exemption, you should be sure your records are
clear and current. The fact that you have the exemption does
not excuse you from filing and showing how you have used the
exemption. If you have rolled over your housing, you should
have a record of the stream of sales and purchases showing
prices and dates. You may add brokerage costs and the cost
of major improvements to your cost basis in order to establish the net gain, but all this takes records. If you cannot find
old records, you will need to recreate them as faithfully as
possible. The IRS is more impressed with contemporaneous
records than with recreated records, but they have been known
to allow recreated records, and the further the date of recre-
ation is away from the date of filing, the more credibility the
records have. If you wait until the last minute, you will have
to hope they believe you. Thus, if you are going to sell your
house near the time of your retirement or during retirement,
now is the time to get the records in place.

To simplify things, I have reduced the alternatives to the
major ones of retaining current housing or moving to alternate
housing. There are variations on each theme, and I examine
them briefly. It is important to recall that this area, like all
others, needs to be integrated into a coherent whole which will
make sense for your retirement. I believe you can be your own
primary financial planner in this area, but I would still rec-

ommend periodic requests for a second opinion from a professional financial planner, and of course you should discuss any contractual changes or changes in your will with your lawyer.

Retain Current Housing

■ *No Change* Many people hope to stay in their current housing until they are no longer able to take care of themselves. There is considerable wisdom in that desire. Roots may be sunk in the local community. Life there is probably more predictable than it would be if you moved, and, while the house itself may be larger than necessary, it may also be largely paid for and well maintained. While staying in the present house with no changes will mean forgoing the benefit of the $125,000 exemption, that may be your choice. In the past, one disadvantage to continuing without change was that a house was the only liquid asset for many academics. Their retirement savings were turned into an annuity over which they had no control, and if they left themselves with a fully invested house, that asset, too, was inflexible. Thus, the only flexibility came through whatever after-tax savings and investments they had been able to acquire. Given the opportunity to cash out retirement savings and use them in your interest, you have more opportunity to put that asset to work in your interests rather than someone else's, so the need to turn your housing into a liquid asset may not be as great as it was for your predecessors. However, many people who stayed in their current housing with no change in financial arrangements for the housing often felt the home become a source of continual and growing expenses: there might be significant remaining mortgage payments; in all likelihood, property taxes would continue to grow; maintenance problems might develop, and as you age, you are less able to do the maintenance yourself; in addition, there are occasional property reassessments which seem to have more to do with politics than an honest appraisal of the value of the property. I know of no way to eliminate all these concerns and remain in the housing unchanged, but there are ways to make changes which may mitigate some of the impact of these events, and you may find one of them sufficiently attractive that you will look upon your housing as a useful asset.

■ *Sell Your House and Rent It Back* One possibility for gaining a steady flow of cash is to sell the property you are presently living in and rent it back from the party to whom you have sold it. This enables you to remain in your house and to enjoy whatever benefits that affords you. It should give you a significant amount of money, depending, of course, on the value of your house, and it has the advantage of taking some burdens off your shoulders. For example, you will not have to deal directly with property tax increases, though, of course that will have to be taken into account in the rent structure. You will not have to worry about maintenance, though someone will. You will transfer homeowner insurance expenses to the new owner, though you should be sure to consider tenants' insurance. You will also gain the advantage of your tax exemption.

The greatest difficulty with this alternative from a financial point of view is finding a willing purchaser. There are financial advantages to the purchaser if he or she has an interest in a rental property. In the first place, the tax deductions you previously had, such as interest on mortgage and property taxes, are transferred to the new owner. In addition, the new owner gets a tax advantage you did not have—a depreciation allowance. In general, rental houses may be depreciated on a 27½ year straight-line basis. Suppose, for example, that your house is worth $137,500. This means that each year, the new owner could claim a deduction of $5,000. That is an advantage which you did not have when you owned the house because it was not a rental property. In addition, someone who is interested in owning and renting *a* property may find this opportunity attractive. You, as a long-time resident of the property, will probably take better care of it than a stranger would. You may intend to live in it for a considerable period of time, thus relieving the new owner from the burden of finding new tenants regularly.

Nonetheless, it is usually difficult to find such a purchaser. Single family homes—even with the depreciation allowance— are not typically considered good investments except in the most high-flying real estate markets. However, if you are interested in this alternative, again careful planning is worthwhile. You might contact both bankers and real estate agents in the area, because they may know of someone who would be interested in such an arrangement. While it may not be the most exotic deal for the purchaser, in general, it is a reasonably safe one. If real estate prices continue to rise faster than inflation, it provides a nice investment vehicle with tax advantages, and, in the right markets, the downside is reasonably well protected.

Some of these arrangements are made within a family. For example, parents sell the house to their children and then rent it back from them. The flow of dollars may be advantageous to both, and it gives the children a solid investment from which they may be able to benefit when they take over. If you are going to leave your house to your children in any event, you might consider this arrangement now. You will need legal and tax expertise before you complete such an arrangement. There is some flexibility in the arrangements for purchase price, rental fee, and so on, but there are limits to that flexibility, and you will have to maintain a businesslike relationship with your children/owners.

The last comment brings up what is, perhaps, the major disadvantage of this possibility when developed among relatives: the intermixing of business and family relationships. Some families seem to be able to handle such situations better than others. Everyone needs to be cool-headed and objective about these arrangements. For example, they may need to consider what should happen in the event of the death of one person— say you or your spouse—and the desire of the other to stay on in the house.

An arrangement which involves family members may be especially appropriate if the people who are to purchase the house want it for their own use after those who are going to rent it no longer need it. Consider, for example, a family homestead in which the children would like to live when the parents leave. In that case, it may make sense to have the younger generation buy the house from the parents and rent it back so the parents can live in it until that is no longer practical, at which time the children can move into it. By purchasing it, the children have it outside estate taxes and probate. That means, also, that further appreciation of the value of the house will not have an impact on the parent's estate. The deed is actually held by the new owners, and your death will make no difference. Your will cannot reverse the procedure and return the house to your estate because you do not have an interest of ownership in it. Thus, your will can no more address it in a legally binding way than it can address the ownership of my house.

Finally, depending upon your financial situation, there is another possibility: that you give your house to your beneficiaries while you are alive. If you can afford to do so, there are some advantages to this alternative. It also has the effect of freezing the value of your house so that it will not continue to appreciate in your estate. It has the effect of relieving you of some expenses such as property taxes, insurance, and maintenance. You can continue to live in the house—though here, too, you need to discuss with your tax and financial planning advisers any rental arrangements. You will have to pay a market-rate rent. However, if it is desirable, under current regulations, the whole transaction probably can be structured so the children can make gifts to you of the difference between the rent and the expenses, which means that from a financial and living point of view, nothing has changed. Again, all that has to be considered in the light of family relationships and should be reviewed *carefully* with your lawyer.

It may be useful to point out that leaving a house to your beneficiaries in your will may not be a favor. Upon your death, your estate has to be settled. Real estate which does not produce income will be valued at its market value. If it cannot be sold in the time allotted by the IRS (currently nine months), your heirs will have to pay the estate tax on its appraised value, which may lead to it being sold at "fire sale" prices. Otherwise, the executor will have to sell more of the liquid assets to cover the estate taxes on the house. The IRS has a time clock; if no decision is made in time, the IRS makes the decision for you. It is a decision which may have significant unfortunate impact on your beneficiaries.

▪ *Reverse Mortgages* Conceptually, reverse mortgages are not difficult to understand. If you have had a mortgage, you effectively borrowed a large sum of money up front, and you have made periodic payments against that sum of money plus interest toward the day when you have paid the mortgage off. You then own the house free and clear. In a reverse mortgage, you are paid a sum of money based on the equity value of your house. In return, the organization or person paying you will own your house after some period of time if payments have been made appropriately. The designation of the time depends upon the provisions of the reverse mortgage. In the extreme, it may be after your death. A host of details must be resolved in the process of making this arrangement. The reverse mortgage business is so new that there are no clear paths or precedents. In a sense, this is similar to selling your property and then renting it back. In this case, however, you receive income based on the value of the house. Generally, you will be selling the house to someone else who does not wish to live in it at the time, but who wants ownership of the house when you leave or die.

Here are some of the issues that need to be resolved:

1. Who holds the deed? Typically, you do, which means it is not exactly like the reverse of a mortgage.
2. Who pays property taxes? Typically, you do, but that is not definite.
3. Who pays for insurance? Typically, you do, though it would make sense to split the insurance. The new owner has a substantial economic interest in making sure that in the event of fire, for example, the dwelling is fully covered at replace-

ment value. You have a substantial economic interest in the contents and in personal living accommodations until you find a new place to live.

4. Who benefits from appreciation in the value of the house? In this case, I differ from many advisers who suggest that you negotiate a provision that you keep the appreciation on the house. If I were the one holding the mortgage, I would not be much interested in the arrangement. When you left or died, I would receive the property at its unappreciated value. While, in some sense, every alternative may have its price, if I were to hold the mortgage, I would charge a substantial amount for you to have that privilege. This, like so many other possibilities, is the kind of issue which can only be solved by looking at numbers and, once again I would suggest doing so with objective advisers.

The basis of the reverse mortgage will be the appraised value of your property at the time you enter into the agreement. The appraiser(s) will examine the property thoroughly and will be interested in the condition of the house as well as any code problems which may be evident. It is best to plan ahead for the appraisal and prepare the house as if you were going to sell it, so that it will be appraised at the highest level possible. This will maximize your eventual income flow.

There is a special type of reverse mortgage with the technical name of *nonrecourse reverse mortgage,* and in the context of this book, it is worth special mention. A nonrecourse reverse mortgage is sometimes called a *reverse-annuity mortgage.* What it does effectively is to turn your ownership of your house into an annuity. Suppose, again, your house is worth $137,500. Suppose the reverse mortgage company is willing to annuitize 80% of its value. You would then have an effective single-premium annuity of $110,000 which would pay out for the remainder of your life and, if you wish, for the life of your named beneficiary. This has all the advantages of an annuity. Another characteristic advantage is that you can decide to sell the house and still recover some of your investment in it, minus, obviously, whatever you have received in the way of payments.

A few years ago, reverse mortgages and reverse annuity mortgages would have been considered exotic financial arrangements. However, they have become more accepted as part of mainstream retirement planning. In June of 1990, the Federal National Mortgage Association announced that it will put up more than two billion dollars for expanding its reverse mortgage program. The American Association of Retired Persons (AARP) has recently endorsed the *concept* of reverse mortgages without, of course, endorsing any particular plan or the notion that such a procedure is appropriate for all people.

The reverse-annuity mortgage preserves your options while giving you dependable income. It also allows you to gain income on a major asset. For budgeting purposes, for example, you might use the funds generated by a reverse annuity mortgage to pay the expenses of the house and thus net out the cost of housing as you enter retirement. In general, however, this is another source of income which may prove to be important to your life-style in retirement. It should not be overlooked.

Changing Housing: Downsizing

■ *Sell Present House and Buy Another* Some people enjoy owning a house. They may think that one way to get some of their investment back out of their house is to sell the house they are living in as they near retirement and buy a smaller house, perhaps in a less expensive area. Sometimes that is possible, and the only way to decide is to look at the numbers. It is important, however, to be careful. Buying remains a long-term commitment, even though the buyer may be in retirement. Be sure you can fit into the new house. After children have grown and left, many people decide to move into a smaller house. You need to know what you are going to do with the things you have accumulated over the years. If you believe you can get rid of most of them, do so before you commit yourself to a smaller space. Practice. Close the doors of some rooms for an extended period of time and see if it is comfortable. What about your books, and so forth? Are you going to give them up? Is there room to build the shelves you will need? What of other collections? It is one thing to say abstractly that you can throw many things away; it is quite another to do without. In the end, all you can do is to perform a careful analysis.

One benefit of selling your house is that you will be able to take advantage of the $125,000 exemption. If you do not sell it, you will lose that benefit. By selling a large expensive house and moving to a less expensive house, you may be able to recover some portion of the money you had tied up in the asset of your original house, and you can use that to supplement your income in retirement. In addition, you may be able to reduce expenses such as property taxes, utilities, and home insurance. Whether these advantages are finally persuasive can only be settled by examining critically all the alternatives.

■ *Sell Present House and Rent Another Place* This is another variation on the downsizing theme. It is another way to receive a financial benefit from your house. The benefits are that you can take advantage of the tax provisions, recover your entire investment in housing, and use the investment as a source of income for your retirement. While it is an option to investigate, it is difficult to recommend it generally as the first thing to do.

In my experience, too many people think that immediately after commencement of the year in which they retire, they will quit their jobs, move into new communities and start living on a reduced income. In general, I think that is probably an unwise set of changes to make simultaneously. They might be smart moves to make over time, but the sudden triple shock may be troublesome both psychologically and financially. As careful as you may have been, you may find that even your best estimating did not turn up enough information about the place to which you intend to move.

Leaving aside the issue of immediate action upon retirement, you are still left with the fact that you may have a house as a primary asset, and you may be interested in ways to make it an income producer rather than a drain on your resources. Selling the house and then renting new quarters is one possible and sensible alternative. Financially, you are no longer attempting to build a pool of money for your retirement. You are now in retirement and trying to live off the income earned from that pool of money. Before retirement, we might have argued that investing in a home is an excellent form of tax-free asset creation; now you no longer need those advantages.

While renting does not eliminate the effects of inflation, it does make your housing costs more predictable. You may sign a lease for a period of time, and some renters are prepared to have multiple-year leases with the rents preprogrammed, thus sharing the risk between landlord and renter. In addition to these financial arguments, many people argue that we have seen the end of the run-up in housing prices. I have already eschewed the role of market prognosticator, so I shall resist the temptation to enter into that debate here. However, given the reduced need for tax sheltering, and the greater need for liquidity, housing is probably not as good an investment in the retirement years as it may have been in previous years.

If you decide ultimately to rent, be sure that the rental space is adequate for your needs. Before signing any lease, be sure to go over it with your financial planner and with your lawyer. Lease provisions are negotiable, and while the prospective landlord may not be willing to bend, many prospective landlords are pleased when prospective tenants look over the lease carefully and discuss it because that means they take it seriously. In short, if you are moving from years of ownership of a house to renting an apartment, be sure you investigate the situation carefully before you move.

Preparation and Maintenance of Your House
Before Retirement

No matter what your ultimate intentions for your housing in retirement, this is a good time to look at the house and consider its physical condition. If you intend to stay in the house, you will want to make it as maintenance-free as possible for your retirement years. If you intend to sell the house, you should begin now to prepare it for sale. If you do that during your preretirement years, your employment income will help pay the costs. In addition, you will be in a much better position to negotiate with contractors and follow up on bad performance or nonperformance. From your point of view, the worst time to deal with contractors is when you are under time pressure. The contractors sense your anxiousness, and they know they can negotiate more favorable terms for themselves. Finally, if you have the work done during your preretirement years, you will be able to enjoy the benefits. Remember if you are going to claim the $125,000 exemption, you may raise the cost basis of your house by whatever amount is put into structural improvements. You cannot use purely cosmetic improvements to raise your cost basis unless you have had them done within six months of the sale of your house. Obviously, determining the difference between structural improvements and purely cosmetic improvements is not an exact science, and, as I indicated previously, it is important to keep careful documentation.

You probably know many of the aspects of your house which need attention. However, many people who are in the process of purchasing a house have found the use of home inspectors to be very helpful. Home inspection is based on an analogy to what the boat industry calls *surveying*. For many years, it has been common for people purchasing a new boat to have a survey done by a professional, often a naval architect. The survey should give the prospective owner a complete analysis of the boat from stem to stern. That practice has made its way into house purchasing; a professional, often an architect, is asked to do a complete analysis of a house. This may be advisable in the early part of your preretirement years. A good home inspector will leave you with an extensive written report which outlines steps required to maintain the structural integrity of the house and its systems. Home inspectors *should* be very critical of the house. One of the advantages to having a comprehensive report is that it enables you to coordinate the work that needs to be done. For example, when you ask plumbers or electricians to do something, you will be able to have them do all the work in one visit. That way, you will not be charged for multiple trips to your house as each problem develops.

I suggest that you have the inspector if you are in your preretirement years and not intending to sell your house soon. If you wait until near the time you want to sell your house, I would caution you about having an inspector. The rules of house-selling still seem to be that the buyer acquires the property "where-is and as-is." However, that harsh doctrine may be going the way of "employment-at-will." If you were to have an inspection near sale time, it is arguable that you would have a legal obligation to disclose the problems identified; it is certainly arguable that you would have a moral obligation to disclose. You will then be in a competitive setting where others will not be disclosing, so you may be selling at a serious disadvantage. However, if the inspection is far enough away from the sale, you will have plenty of time to attend to any issues it uncovers.

It is worth noting that the legal situation of selling houses seems to be changing quite substantially. Increasingly, prospective purchasers are using home inspectors. I think they should and would recommend that if you have decided to use the alternative of downsizing by purchasing a smaller house. In addition, there seems to be a growing tendency to suggest that if you were to sell someone a house which was out of code, whether you know it or not, you will be held responsible even well after the consummation of the sale. In California and Maine, everyone who sells a house must identify in writing any defects in the house they know about and must disclose potential areas of difficulty. Real estate agents have become concerned about suits launched against them as coconspirators in selling houses in a bad condition. Consequently, in June of 1990, the National Association of Realtors began a national campaign designed to force all people who sell private houses to identify any defects they know about and to disclose potential areas of difficulty they may not have examined. NAR has a reputation as one of the most effective lobbies in Washington, and people predict that they are likely to be successful in getting supportive legislation. Such legislation would effectively legally exempt real estate agents from any culpability, and it would all fall on the shoulders of the seller.

The best way to deal with these problems and others which may follow is to have a careful and comprehensive plan in mind for the preretirement years so that the retirement years can be as free of stress as possible.

6

Retirement and Early Postretirement Planning

Introduction

As your retirement becomes imminent, you must make some decisions and take some actions to support you in retirement. If you are going to manage your own investments, I shall presume that you have prepared for retirement in many of the ways suggested. You should have accumulated a significant retirement savings pool which you believe will be adequate to support you during retirement. I shall assume those funds will be divided between a fixed income and a growth orientation roughly in accordance with the age-to-fixed-income allocation general rule I suggested. If they are not, or if they have gotten out of balance, this may be a good time to ask yourself whether you wish to continue with the different ratio. Variations may be made in accordance with your own sense of longevity. If you have had regular medical checkups, you have no health problems, and you come from a gene pool with a history of longevity, you may wish to shade that proportion lower so you have more in equities in order to stay ahead of inflation for a longer period of time. If, however, you have serious health problems and your gene pool shows little longevity, you may want to shade the allocation higher to be sure your portfolio is safely generating an income adequate to your needs. You may also take into account your own sense of the economy and the strength of your belief in your ability to predict the economy.

While there is little evidence that people can predict long-term movements in the economy precisely, you may think you have a more reliable sense of where the economy is headed over a shorter term, and (again, depending on your health) your time horizon may be short. If you have a sense that the economy is stalled and that even if it moves forward, there will not be a robust expansion in your lifetime, you may want to shade the allocation toward fixed income. If, however, you think the economy is poised waiting for a significant expansion sometime in the early part of the remainder of your lifetime, you may want to shade toward emphasis on the equity portion. Predicting the economy may be like predicting the weather: short-term predictions are the most reliable, and long-term precise predictions are almost useless. If you are right down the middle on your health—as much reason for longevity as for caducity—and if you are right down the middle on the future of the economy in your lifetime—as much reason for pessimism as for optimism—the age-to-allocation formulation should be adequate to the occasion.

In addition, I shall assume that you have diversified your savings funds roughly in accordance with the general rule of keeping no less than $100,000 and no more than $200,000 under any single management supervision. Again, I can imagine circumstances in which it would be wise to deviate from the suggestion.

If you have not followed these general rules, you will have to make some adjustments in the subsequent analyses in this chapter. I do not think those adjustments will be extensive, but you may need to remember them as you read the chapter. I shall assume, also, that you have made some decisions about housing in retirement and that you are prepared to put those plans into operation.

You should determine if you should spend any of your retirement savings as a capital expenditure. For example, some people may decide to eliminate their mortgage or satisfy some other lingering debt. Others may wish to make some substantial home improvements in order to lower expenses later. Still others may decide the beginning of retirement is a time to purchase an automobile which may carry them through retirement. An endless list of possibilities exists for major expenditures, and I am not suggesting that such expenditures should be made at this time. The decisions should be basically economic ones. If the expenditure has an actual payback in the next two or three years, it may make sense. However, expenditures of this nature merely to make retirement more pleasant need to be examined carefully. It is just because the surrogate parents of academics were sure that we would squander our retirement savings that they set up systems to prevent cashing out. However, there *are* cases of rational decisions in this regard, and it is just as foolish to refuse to make them as it would be to waste money. I suggest discussions with a fee-only financial planner—an objective but supportive outsider. If the planner is convinced by your arguments for a major expenditure, perhaps it *is* advisable. If the planner shows you the holes in your rationalizations, perhaps you should rethink the issue. Part of your calculation should involve understanding the tax consequences of what you are considering. You will have to pay regular income taxes on tax-sheltered money received, and receiving it in large sums while you are taking distributions for regular income purposes may put you in a higher tax bracket. That would mean the marginal cost of those dollars would be higher than otherwise. In addition, you and your planner should be careful not to put you over the maxima established by Social Security, threatening your social security distributions. Once again, thinking and planning ahead are the clues to resolving these issues satisfactorily.

At this stage, two sets of questions must be faced directly. The first has to do with how you should receive your income in your retirement. The recent changes give you more alternatives, and some of that flexibility may be important to you. The second set of questions has to do with your medical care in your retirement. This chapter will discuss both sets of questions and suggest the issues which you will need to address. I continue to recommend avoiding an approach which forces you to experience a series of lurches both into retirement and beyond. My ideal is that through planning you can have a reasonably smooth transition which is marked by a few unavoidable, irreversible decisions. Retirement itself is one of those irreversible decisions.

In terms of receiving retirement income, my general suggestion is that you will probably find it advantageous to use a combination of annuities and self-management, and that the appropriate combination of the two will change over time. For example, in general, I would not suggest that people who are retiring early should use annuities as the primary source of their income. In the first place, the younger you are when you initiate an annuity contract, the smaller the payments will be. In the second place, if you are retiring at fifty-five, for example, and if you are healthy, we can reasonably expect that you may live another twenty-five or thirty years. The economy can go through major twists and turns in that period of time, and I think you would be wise to maintain substantial control over the source of your income stream during that period. A brief glance at the thirty years from 1960 to 1990 reveals how dramatic and unpredictable the changes in the economy may be. I have no reason to believe the changes in the next thirty years will not be as unpredictable and dramatic. On the other hand, the older you are when you retire, or the later you are in your retirement, the more attractive the annuity rates should be, and the more comfortable you may feel living on an income stream over which you have little control. Thus, I suggest that whereas at fifty-five, your income might come primarily from self-management, at eighty-five, your income might come primarily from annuities. On these grounds, in the intervening years, there might be a gradual shift from self-management to annuities. Once again, what I suggest is merely a rule of thumb. I can easily imagine particular circumstances in which there are very good reasons for deviating both ways from the rule.

Social Security Income

Social security payments will not start automatically upon your retirement even if you have regularly used the Social Security Administration's services for obtaining estimates on your social security income. You must apply for social security payments to start, and it is wise to begin that process four to six months before you plan to retire. For example, if you are planning to retire just after a spring commencement, the first of the calendar year is a good time to make the initial contacts with the Social Security Administration office near you. I have found them to be responsive and helpful, but, as with any enormous bureaucracy, everything takes longer than we would like. The earlier you start, the more relaxed you can be, and the more cooperative they are likely to be.

Annuities

Since, until the changes, annuities were the only alternative, it makes sense to consider them first in this context. The last chapter outlined many of the alternatives and the analyses which you should make. I also suggested that you diversify your placement of annuities roughly in accordance with the suggestion for diversification of your retirement savings. I shall assume you have done the appropriate analyses. You now need to make a decision as to what proportion of your retirement income you want generated initially by annuities. I suggested a rule of thumb in the previous paragraphs, and I shall assume you have made that decision, also.

You should also watch the timing of your annuity payments so there will be no lengthy unbroken stretch of time without an income. All that is left, then, is the mechanical act of filling out the forms and being sure you sign up for the contract you want. The representatives of the financial organizations, including TIAA-CREF, are likely to be cooperative and helpful in completing the process and making sure it goes smoothly.

Self-Management

Converting Savings to After-Tax Dollars

You *may* convert your entire retirement savings pool into after-tax dollars by taking it directly. If you elect to do that, you must begin a carefully structured program to do it, and you may not change course in mid-stream. There is an explicit IRS provision which allows you to do that and calculate taxes due by forward averaging over a five-year period. That means that instead of paying income taxes on the total sum in one year, you are allowed to allocate the sum over five years. That *may* keep you in a lower tax bracket, so that some of the dollars would be received at a lower marginal tax rate, which means overall you will have more after-tax money. However, this is all based on the assumption that you will receive it at the lower rate and that the tax rate will not rise during the five years. I would find those political predictions to be very uncertain. It is important to remember, however, that once you take the money and pay taxes on it, you will have to pay taxes on anything it earns subsequently. I do not think it would be wise to attempt to negotiate such a distribution alone. If you are prepared to bring yourself up to date on the *current* tax regulations, you might continue to treat yourself as the first opinion and seek a second opinion from professionals. As this is being written, the regulations are complex but not lengthy, and as far as I know, thus far there are no cases which require attention for interpretation. As with all tax matters, however, the entire territory can change almost overnight. I would not make such arrangements without a second opinion. In general, this procedure of taking the money directly is only advisable where the funds will be used within a few years. If the funds are to be held for a number of years, the tax advantages of the tax-free environment are likely to outweigh the advantages of converting the funds to an after-tax basis.

I can think of three different conditions in which taking the money as a lump-sum on a forward-averaging basis could prove attractive:

1. You are very sure that in the near future you are going to inherit a substantial sum which will provide the basis for your income after that, and you want to start living the good life now.
2. You are convinced that you are going to die in the next few years, and you want the funds to enjoy life as fully as possible before that.
3. You are entering a lifetime care community (see chapter 7), and you need the money for your entrance fee.

You cannot go half way. If you leave part of your 403(b) retirement savings money and do not take it as after-tax money, you cannot use the five-year forward averaging feature. I do not think this approach will prove to be advantageous to many people.

If you are going to manage some of the retirement savings yourself, as you make the final preparations for retirement, you will have to make decisions about the manner in which you intend to withdraw money from your retirement savings in order to have an adequate income for retirement. The issues are the ones which I indicated would prevail throughout: you do not want to outlive your source of adequate income, and yet you want to be sure to keep up with inflation. Another issue is important. If you have developed an appropriate portfolio and allocation policy, you do not want to disturb that in order to provide your income. Further, recall my suggestion that the total distribution might average out to three-quarters of the retirement income (in retirement-time dollars), but you will probably want to have something close to your preretirement income upon initial retirement and allow that to decline as your needs decline. Before we turn to the formulation of a useful system, we should understand how the self-managed retirement savings funds are to be handled after retirement.

Withdrawal Policies for Self-Managed Funds

You may cash out your funds and maintain the tax-free environment as you begin to use the funds to support your retirement. There is a specific IRS provision for the transfer of 403(b) money to an IRA which is labeled a *Rollover IRA*. The transfer may involve setting up new accounts, and sometimes it can be accomplished merely by the redesignation of the investment funds. The rules for receiving the money, then, follow the rules of IRAs. In general, nothing may be taken without penalty before age 59½ and some funds must start to be taken by age 70½. The funds which remain—even those which remain after 70½—are still allowed to accumulate in a tax-free environment. Of course, you must pay income taxes on any money withdrawn from the rollover IRA. If you move funds, they must be reinvested within sixty days of their withdrawal. In general, funds already in mutual funds other than TIAA-CREF do not need to be disturbed, since they are already in place. TIAA-CREF also has some provision for continuation and periodic withdrawal. You need to communicate with the representatives of your financial organizations and tell them of your intentions, so that you can complete the appropriate paperwork before you start your retirement. Many organizations are willing to put you on a defined payout schedule and send you periodic checks as you direct, but that usually requires you to complete additional forms. The primary question you must answer is how much you should withdraw as you use the returns on these investments to support your income.

I think there are five important criteria for determining appropriate withdrawal policies for your retirements savings.

1. Your total income from all sources (annuities, social security, outside income, savings, reverse mortgages, etc.) should allow you to retire at close to your immediate pre-retirement income, and over time you should expect a decline to something between one-half and three-fourths the initial income in uninflated dollars.

2. Your withdrawal policy should insure as far as possible that you neither outlive your income nor find the purchasing power of your income deteriorating as a result of inflation.
3. You should suffer no extraordinary tax penalties as a result of your policies.
4. Your withdrawal policy should establish an objective amount to withdraw which is not subject to *ad hoc* adjustments as a result of momentary whims. The great danger of self-management is that we will not have the requisite self-discipline, and that after a period of nibbling away at our funds, we shall find them inadequate.
5. Your withdrawal policy should be independent of both your investment and your allocation policies. Those policies should be based on good investment strategies and should not be changed to generate enough dividends and interest to support your income demands. In the endowment-management world, this is known as a total return, and it acquired a bad reputation when it was first proposed. However, I think it makes good sense. If your investment policy is driven by what you consider as your needs, you will end up with a bad investment policy, a bad allocation policy, and a bad withdrawal policy.

While the future is unpredictable, and no plan can be foolproof, there is a withdrawal policy which will meet all five criteria if you have prepared for and timed your retirement as suggested. I recommend a program by which the annual portion of your savings which you withdraw is computed by dividing the total amount of your savings by your life expectancy. Useful life expectancy tables are available from the IRS, and they are included in two IRS publications: #575, *Pension and Annuity Income* and #590, *Individual Retirement Accounts*. If you are married and the distribution is to cover both of you, the tables allow for a combined life expectancy calculation on a unisex basis. That combined life expectancy is greater than a single life expectancy. There is an additional dividend from adopting such a withdrawal policy because IRS regulations require that once you have reached age 70½, you *must* begin a withdrawal program for your IRAs, and the amounts indicated by this suggested policy are the *minimal* amounts you must withdraw.

Whether or not you decide to retire before 70½, I think this withdrawal policy is a workable one. For example, if you are considering retirement at age 62, you could use life expectancy calculations for 62 to calculate the amount you would consider withdrawing. The amount calculated in this manner should then be compared to the amount determined by your declining-need calculation. You should subtract the amount provided by sources other than retirement savings (e.g., Social Security) to arrive at the amount needed from your retirement savings.

If the amount thus calculated is greater than you need and if you are less than 70½ years old, then you simply should not take the extra amount from your IRA. If the amount calculated is greater than you need and if you are over 70½ years old, then you should take the extra amount, pay taxes on it (which is the IRS's interest), and save the extra amount in an after-tax savings account.

If, in any case, it is less than the amount you need, you should take the lesser amount and trim your needs to fit. However, if that should occur, it would mean that you did not do the appropriate calculating before retiring. Those calculations should have revealed to you that you could not afford to retire when you did. Once again, it is very important to plan ahead in regard to all these issues. You may not be able to afford to retire as soon as you wish. You may wish to look again at your needs during retirement. There are a number of alternatives to consider, and nothing suggests that they will all come out positive for retirement at a specific age. The longer you wait to retire, the easier it will be to support your retirement through self-management or through an annuity. These issues have to be decided on an individual basis, but at least *we* can decide them. During my years as an administrator, one of the most distressing responsibilities I placed on myself was talking with faculty and administrators who had been forced into retirement and had been forced to accept one of the annuity options offered by TIAA-CREF, but still did not have adequate funds to live a decent life. There were—and still are—heart-rending cases out there.

Two final points should be made about this suggestion. First, remember that even though you must begin receiving your income at 70½, you do not have to retire then. Second, remember that even though you must *begin* receiving your income at 70½, the rest of the funds in your retirement savings continue to earn in a tax-free environment.

Acute Medical Care

I have suggested that the twin fears in retirement are inadequate financial resources and inadequate provisions for medical care. This section deals with issues of providing adequate medical care insofar as what is called *acute medical care* is concerned.

A terminological distinction should be made in order to distinguish the treatment of medical concerns in this chapter from their treatment in the next chapter. In this chapter, I am concerned primarily with what is called *acute* medical care. The word *acute* is chosen to indicate that health care professionals believe the problem will yield to medical intervention and treatment, that the medical care has curative and rehabilitative purpose, and that at the conclusion of the care, the patient will be able to return to a reasonably independent life. In the next chapter, I shall analyze provisions for long-term custodial medical care.

Those who suspect the difference between acute medical care and long-term custodial care is a difference in degree rather than a difference in kind are right, and the overlap areas will be discussed also. However, it is not wise to depend upon using that overlap as a means of covering both conditions at half the price. Some patients and their families mistakenly try to stretch the acute-care coverage to include long-term custodial coverage, only to find too late that the distinctions will be strictly enforced. Except in very unusual circumstances, you will need both forms of coverage, and you will probably use both forms sometime in your retirement.

Early Retirement

As I pointed out in the section on "Planning Retirement Timing" in chapter 5, if you plan to retire early (i.e., before sixty-five), it is very important that you understand precisely what medical coverage will be available to you. In general, if you retire before you can receive Social Security payments, Medicare will not be available to you until you reach sixty-five. We all need to understand fully what our medical care provisions will be; that is doubly true for those who retire early.

Retirement After Sixty-five

After sixty-five, there are fundamentally three different ways to deal with acute health care issues: Medicare, health maintenance organizations (HMOs), and lifetime care communities. They are not mutually exclusive; one might be selected for one period and another in a later period. Once again, it is useful to make the point that retirement is not a single homogeneous time in the life of the retiree. There will be a progression of events, and it may make some sense to move along that progression in a paced way rather than lurching from one phase to another.

Medicare

■ *Medicare: Plan A* Plan A in Medicare covers partial payments for hospital stays and services. It is sometimes referred to as Hospital Insurance (HI). I shall not describe the details of the coverage or its limits; such a description would be beyond the scope of this book, and the information is readily available. A good university benefits office should have the appropriate information. You should also be able to find it in a library, and if it is not there, a Social Security Office will send you the information.

While Medicare Plan A covers an important portion of hospitalization costs, it does not cover all of them. What are referred to as *copayments* (i.e., the amounts it will not cover) can mount quickly and substantially. The later section on medigap insurance, suggests how to deal with these problems. One of the many misconceptions about Medicare is that once a person is covered by it, there will be no more medical expense problems.

On the first day of the month in which you turn sixty-five, if you are eligible for social security payments, you are automatically eligible for Medicare. It is important to note that you are *eligible;* that does not mean you will automatically have coverage. The only way you can be put under Medicare automatically is if your social security payments also begin on your sixty-fifth *birthday.* In that case, your application for social security payments will be treated automatically as an application for Medicare. In all other circumstances, you must apply directly for Medicare. Since you will probably not retire on the first day of the month in which you turn sixty-five, you will probably have to apply directly for Medicare. If you are going to retire after commencement in the year you become sixty-five, you should apply for Medicare four to six months before your birthday. You may do that at the same time you apply for Social Security, but the forms are different, and it is not the same process.

If you are covered by university health insurance, that coverage will normally continue after you turn sixty-five until you retire. As long as you have not retired, your university health insurance should be your primary provider and Medicare should be a secondary provider, picking up where the university coverage leaves off and where Medicare would still make payments. After sixty-five *and retirement,* Medicare will be your primary acute medical insurance coverage. Effectively, you have no choice but to participate in Plan A when you turn sixty-five.

Plan A used to be fully paid for when users became sixty-five. However, there is now a supplemental premium due, depending upon your income tax level. For example, in 1992, you will be charged $40.50 per year for each $150 of your federal income tax up to a maximum of $950 per year. That amount is scheduled to rise rapidly in the next years.

■ *Medicare: Plan B*   You have an opportunity to elect to participate in Plan B of Medicare, which is designed to cover a portion of physicians' fees for acute medical care. Participation in Plan B is voluntary. Even so, Plan B does not cover the entire physicians' fees, nor does it cover fees for routine check-ups, and so forth. The euphemism used here is that it will cover "reasonable" physicians' fees. Reasonableness is operationally defined by fee schedules established by the Social Security Administration.

Some physicians agree to accept what are called *assignments*, which means they agree to accept the Plan B reimbursements as specified. In these cases, the physician's office asks you to sign a form indicating that the procedure was carried out, and it bills Medicare directly. Medicare reimburses the physician for 80% of its established fee; you are responsible for the remaining 20%. You do not have to be involved beyond that. Your Social Security office should have a list of physicians in your area who accept assignment.

I have never seen a study attempting to determine whether physicians on assignment render better medical services than those not on assignment. However, there is a strong prevailing opinion that physicians who charge more are better medically. No solid evidence I know of supports or defeats that hypothesis. In economics, this phenomenon is sometimes referred to as a *kinky* demand curve (i.e., demand actually *rises* with a rise in price), and I think it occurs more often than conventional economics concedes.

It is very important for you to determine where your physician stands in regard to assignment and the payment of fees. Some physicians will accept assignment on a blanket basis. Some will accept the assignment fees but only on an *ad hoc* basis. Some will not accept them at all. You need to make balanced judgments for yourself about physicians and finances while you are well, not while you are in need of acute medical care. There is one other complication: physicians who do not accept assignment on a blanket basis do not bill Medicare directly. They bill you directly, and it is your responsibility to try to recover from Medicare. In my experience, the physicians' offices are usually very helpful in this process, but the burden is yours nonetheless, and if you do not carry it out, you will end up paying the entire bill yourself. In addition, being responsible yourself for recovering the money means that there is likely to be a substantial time delay for you in receiving your funds. I have heard about "normal" time delays of up to one year. You are out the money, and you lose the use of that money and what it might earn to help your retirement. There was new legislation passed in December of 1990 which *seems* to put the burden of recovering from Medicare on the shoulders of all the physicians, but that legislation has not been tested in the courts yet, nor has it been tested in practice. Until there is more experience with it, I would suggest caution.

You have a choice about participating in Plan B, and you have a decision to make. If your university medical coverage is appropriate, you will not need the coverage of Plan B while you are employed. If you purchase it, you will probably be doubly insured and will probably gain no additional benefit. As long as enrollment in Plan B is completed within seven months of your *retirement*, there will be no penalty for late enrollment. However, after that there will be a penalty which is calculated using a twelve-month-unit basis. They will count each twelve-month period in which you *could* have been covered by Plan B but did not choose to be covered (including the seven-month grace period just referenced). They will then multiply the number of those periods by 10%. The resulting percentage will then be added to your Plan B premium to calculate your new premium. The penalty remains in effect for the duration of the time you are enrolled in Plan B.

In order to understand the implications of the penalty, I shall use a simplified example. In 1991, the monthly premium for Plan B was approximately $30.00. That premium can be adjusted annually. For the sake of the example, suppose you turned sixty-five in 1991 and retired in June of 1991 after commencement. Suppose, further that you decided not to participate in Plan B until after July of 1994, three twelve-month periods later. For the sake of arithmetical simplicity, suppose the premiums on Plan B had not increased. *Your* premium for Plan B would be $39.00 each month. Thus, by not signing up for Plan B upon retirement, you would have saved $1,080. Leaving aside the effects of inflation, in ten more years, you will have broken even. Thus, if you expect to live at least thirteen years, which is shorter than your actuarial life expectancy, you will have come out ahead. Notice, however, there is a hidden assumption that you will have suffered no coverable medical problem in the three-year interlude. If you suffered any, the difference will have to be taken into account, and physicians' bills can accumulate quickly.

Finally, you should recognize that Plan B does not cover all costs; the copayment principle remains in effect. Even where physicians accept assignment, you will have to pay 20% of their fees. Thus, both Plan A and Plan B leave what are called *gaps* in medical insurance, and there are programs to close those gaps—usually at your expense.

■ *Medigap Insurance*   The term *medigap* is a generic term indicating what some private insurance programs are intended to accomplish. It is a reference to a kind of insurance, not the name of an insurance program as Medicare and Medicaid are. The general purpose of medigap insurance is to close the gaps created by the difference between the medical coverage which is typically provided before retirement and the coverage provided through Medicare in retirement. Medigap insurance is provided by private insurance companies, not by the government. The policies vary considerably, as do medical policies covering employees. It is important to understand the provisions, especially as you are entering into retirement, because it will be much more difficult to make up for any financial setbacks, whether they are caused by medical problems or other problems.

The more enlightened universities permit faculty to continue to participate in the health insurance programs which the universities sponsored before the faculty members retired—at the faculty member's expense. The *most* enlightened pay for that participation. Corporations routinely pay for coverage for their retired executives, but many board members I have known often react to analogous proposals for us as if they amounted to something between legalized embezzling and socialized medicine.

If your university permits such continuing participation, be sure to examine its provisions carefully (they are not uniform), and, as a rebuttable presumption, I would suggest that you accept it even though you may have to pay for it. If your university does not provide it, you may be able to obtain such insurance on the open market. You need to examine that alternative early in case there are preexisting condition clauses, and you need to look at the benefits and the expenses. As of November, 1991, federal legislation has mandated that people looking for medigap insurance cannot be turned down for preexisting conditions if it is their first medigap coverage and if they apply within six months of becoming *eligible* for Medicare, Part B. That may provide some protection, and I hope it reinforces the need to make careful preparations for your actual retirement. Since the legislation is so new, since it has not been tested, and since there are a number of conditions for its coverage, I do not suggest that you let your guard down in your efforts to understand all requirements and investigate all situations carefully. However, this information may be useful if you should be told by some provider about provisions for not covering preexisting conditions.

Remember, the purpose of insurance is to pool risks and provide support for people in regard to losses they cannot withstand individually. The more you attempt to close gaps which you will be able to afford, the higher the premiums are likely to be, and the more you will be wasting money. You can accept deductibles at low ends, and it is usually to your advantage to do so. Proportionately, it costs the insurance company much less to process a claim for thousands of dollars as a result of surgery and a hospital stay than it does to process a claim for $20.00 worth of prescription drugs. Medicare does not pay for prescription drugs, so if you try to find insurance to close that gap entirely, the insurance policy offering it will recover the costs of processing it in your premium. Like the service contract on a new appliance, it may make you feel good when you need the service, but it is probably a waste of money.

During the 1970s and into the 1980s, some people suggested that retirees could save money by "going naked," as they called it. That usually meant not purchasing medigap insurance, though some even suggested going naked in regard to Plan B. I do not advise that. Medical bills can mount so fast and become so dramatic that they alone can spoil all other plans you can make. This is an area for the insurance function and, while the premiums are not low, after you have retired is no time to be going naked.

Four final points are worthy of mention. First, details are very important. You need to understand precisely what Medicare will provide, what its limitations are, and how—if at all—your university's extended policy will cover the gaps. There is no substitute for a careful examination. Either your university's benefits office, the library, or the local Social Security office will have the necessary information on Medicare. Your benefits office should have information on coverage offered under its auspices. While it is helpful to have people explain policies and provisions to you, be sure you have written information of an official nature.

Second, the entire situation is complicated and made more complicated than necessary by the insurance people themselves. Medicare has provisions for appeal, and I would suggest using them. A high percentage of appeals are eventually approved. I have wondered on occasion whether the structure is already set up to render the highest bill and then wait for an appeal. People who accept the highest bill are then out of luck, but they do not know it; people who appeal successfully feel good about the system. The offices are to be congratulated for listening to consumer problems and complaints, but, if I may extrapolate from my experience, it is unfortunate that their accounts are rendered inaccurately too often. As this chapter was being written, the press reported that millions of senior citizens below the $6,620 annual income poverty line have been charged for Medicare payments in spite of legislation passed the previous year which required the federal government to pay Plan B premiums for such people. When the problem was brought to light, it seems the official explanation was that since many of those people failed to apply for the benefit, they did not receive it. This illustrates that we need to be prepared to take an active role in order to receive the correct benefits. I suggest that you learn what the appeal process requires and take advantage of it. If your bill is substantial, if you are convinced you are right, and if you lose at the first level of appeal, you might consider outside help in the form of a lawyer, but that can be expensive and may not be justified except in extreme cases.

Third, the whole medical care situation is undergoing debate and change currently. In many ways, it seems that the only thing the experts and the politicians can agree on is that the current national health care system is in need of substantial overhaul. It is impossible to predict what may come out of the debates, but if you are approaching retirement, it is important to follow them, so that you will understand the impact on your own situation.

Fourth, you should be careful about the financial health of the medical insurance company supporting any medigap insurance. The library should have a listing of the reports which assess the strength of insurance companies. They are published by the same corporations which assess the strength of insurance companies offering annuities, and, once again, it is wise to stay with the insurance companies which receive the two highest ratings. Given the instability in the insurance business, even among highly rated companies, you should keep check regularly on the financial health of your medical insurance carrier.

Health Maintenance Organizations

A second way to deal with medical expenses is by joining a health maintenance organization (HMO). These organizations were created in the 1960s and 1970s in an effort to bring medical costs under some control. From the patient's point of view, they have the advantage of providing a kind of "one-stop-shopping" medical care without the billing. In the typical HMO situation, you or your university will pay a set fee which covers all your acute care medical needs; the only charges to you are very modest copayments which are primarily nuisance payments. Usually the easiest way to get into an HMO is through your university medical coverage plan, though some allow individual entrance. Federal regulations now require that if employers offer medical insurance to their employees, they must offer HMO opportunities where that is available. The employer must pay the HMO an amount at least equivalent to what they pay other providers in policy premiums. The employee may have to pay any differences. Universities and university faculty were among the leaders of the HMO movement, and they maintain a close relationship.

In regard to Plan B coverage, you indicate to Social Security that you are insured with an HMO when you sign up, and Medicare pays the HMO for all services at the rates covered under Medicare. In some cases, the HMO covers more than required by Medicare, but it may not cover less. Thus, the coverage remains whether you subscribe to an HMO or through a medical insurance company.

One of the disadvantages of HMOs is that they do not exist everywhere, so you may find it inappropriate in your particular circumstance. Another disadvantage is that you have less choice in regard to physicians, and you cannot look around as easily, though most HMOs allow you to exercise some preference for the physicians you want as long as they are on the HMO staff. Some people worry about coverage with an HMO if they are not in the geographic area when their acute medical problem arises. That is, of course, a cause for *concern*. I have never known of an HMO which did not willingly provide coverage for services rendered in a place outside its geographic area if an emergency were involved. However, it is an issue worth examining and one which would warrant looking closely at the rules and regulations as well as talking to patients who have used the HMO. Be sure to read all documentation carefully. You do not want to try to understand the rules and procedures just as you are in acute pain and all your energy is absorbed in dealing with your illness.

One great advantage of HMOs is that you do not have to appeal bills. The charges are absorbed in the structure of the system. However, a parallel disadvantage is that you may have to appeal medical decisions. Suppose, for example, you had an unusual problem, and you know that a leading expert on that disease practices nearby. Your plan administrators and the physicians' committee might decide they could treat the problem themselves without spending the money to pay that other physician. Suppose, then, that you or your relatives disagree with their medical judgment. You would have a serious problem just at a time you did not want it. You could call in the other physician at your expense, but you would have no insurance coverage. The fact that the HMO's physicians' committee is not likely to condone unethical medical treatment and the fact that you are probably wrong may be scant comfort if you are suffering and if you are convinced that some other physician could stop your suffering.

In considering HMOs, you should also consider carefully the financial viability of the particular HMO. HMOs have had financial problems in the past, and you certainly do not want to get into one which goes out of business, though I do not know of any which have gone out of business and left participants without coverage. I have known about HMOs in financial difficulty which were subsequently taken over by other healthy HMOs to no detriment of the participants in either plan. However, just because no HMO I know about has gone out of business does not mean none of them can go out of business. It is very unusual for a college or university to go out of business, also, but it has happened, and people have been seriously hurt in the process. I think you should be sure to examine the HMO's financial stability carefully, and I think you should ask about any contingency plans in case the HMO should have bad financial experience. While you have considerably more flexibility to respond in the face of financial problems with your medical insurance carrier than you would with your annuity carrier, there could be significant problems if your HMO were to close suddenly. Other potential carriers may insist on eliminating any preexisting conditions from coverage.

A Preliminary Reference to Lifetime Care Communities

A third way for dealing with health care in this context is through what I call *lifetime care communities*. They provide an approach which more fully integrates acute medical care and long-term custodial care, though their emphasis is on the latter. Consequently, I shall save discussion of them until the next chapter. It is possible that over the period of your retirement, you may wish to combine either the Medicare approach or the HMO approach with the use of lifetime care communities.

Part Four

Decisions in Retirement

7

Midretirement Planning

Allocation and Adequacy of Savings

The midretirement period is a time for taking stock of how your retirement planning is working and whether adjustments are needed. The early years of retirement should have proceeded successfully, but now you will begin to experience the effect of the decline in real dollar income. If you have taken care of your significant needs in the previous planning, you should not have trouble with the decline in income because your needs should have declined also. If you decided to manage some of your retirement savings yourself, you should examine the allocation between fixed income and equities to be sure that you have made the appropriate adjustments using as a rule of thumb the age-to-percent-of-fixed-income formulation. As you become older, you will have less time to make up for dips in the equity markets, and you will be increasingly interested in making sure that your income is maintained. In addition, as you grow older, you will not have to worry as much about the ravages of inflation. You may also have a clearer sense of your health and how that will affect your longevity. You should make adjustments as you see fit. It might make some sense to meet again with your fee-only financial planner to be sure that you have not missed anything.

You may find that while previously you have been willing to manage some important segment of your retirement savings yourself, you no longer wish to put the same energy into that job. That may incline you to look again at the possibility of professional investment counseling or of purchasing annuities.

Annuities

The presumption of much generic retirement planning seems to be that the time to take out annuities is at the point of retirement. That advice is at least questionable. The appropriate use of annuities is probably much more a function of your age and health than it is of your employment condition. As you approach the midretirement period (for example, your middle to late seventies), in general, it may make sense to increase your commitment to annuities. You may wish to be free of some of the burdens of managing your own money, and you probably have a clearer idea of the resources you may need for the remainder of your life. Furthermore, as I have pointed out previously, the terms of annuities become more attractive the older you are.

I should reemphasize that while purchasing annuities is an irreversible decision, the decisions do not have to be of a completely either/or nature. As suggested earlier, you might decide to phase your retirement funds toward annuities, retaining some management for yourself and placing increasing amounts in annuities. The age-ratio for your investments makes sense for the allocation of your purchase of fixed versus variable annuities. For example, if you are seventy-five, your annuities might be about 75% fixed and about 25% variable. You can accomplish that by taking the appropriate proportional amounts out of your retirement savings. As you age, if you continue to purchase annuities, you let that ratio shade more toward a higher proportion of fixed annuities by purchasing proportionally more of them.

Once again, there is a clear advantage to not moving entirely into annuities at retirement. You maintain much more flexibility over your retirement program, and you can adjust it to suit your particular needs. For example, people who are in excellent health at seventy-five might sensibly adopt a different program from those whose probable longevity is shorter. In the extreme, if you are in declining health, you should probably not purchase any more annuities.

The issues in regard to annuities in general have not changed since the discussion of annuities in chapter 5. The most important thing to do is to look at the alternatives and make a decision based on what is appropriate for you. As you invest increasing proportions of your retirement savings in annuities, be sure to stay with the highly rated financial institutions and to diversify your purchases among financial institutions. There is no panacea for a risk-free retirement. Caution and diversification are the best approaches.

Long-Term Medical Care

Myth

Some people believe that Medicare will cover their long-term health and custodial care needs. That is not true. As indicated in the last chapter, Medicare is designed to cover acute medical problems which are curable. For example, Medicare covers nursing home needs specifically only under very limited conditions. I shall outline those conditions briefly, but I emphasize that they are *meant* to be exclusive, so the guardhouse lawyers who think they can find a loophole should read the original regulations and consult with a lawyer before depending on that opportunity. The conditions follow:

1. The treatment must be short-term and of a definable period, to be reviewed if its curative objective is not accomplished.
2. The treatment must be medically justified as curative or recovery-oriented.

3. The patient must have been assigned—legitimately—to a hospital for at least three days prior to entering the nursing home.
4. The hospitalization must have been for the same problem which led to reassignment to the nursing home.
5. Entry into the nursing home must occur within thirty days of hospitalization.
6. While in the nursing home, the patient must need around-the-clock, daily skilled nursing care for rehabilitation.
7. The patient must enter into a Medicare approved *skilled* nursing home (the word *skilled* is a technical term designated for these purposes by Medicare).
8. The seven conditions above must *all* be met.

If you have the impression that the purpose is to provide an inexpensive alternative to lengthy hospitalization rather than a way for patients to have Medicare pay for their nursing home stay, you are right. If, for example, you have a heart attack and are assigned by your physician to a skilled nursing home for rehabilitative medicine after your hospitalization, as long as you are making noticeable and steady progress toward your recovery, Medicare will probably cover some of your nursing home care costs. If, however, you are in advanced stages of Parkinson's disease and must enter a nursing home for your own safety and well-being, your stay will probably not be covered by Medicare.

Medicare is designed for acute medical care, not custodial care. However, as the aging process continues, it becomes more likely that custodial care is what you will need. Perhaps the fact that less than 5% of the nursing home assignments are covered by Medicare will make my point clear. As medical science continues to make progress, more people are likely to die from conditions caused by the body wearing out than from acute crises. To put the matter another way, acute crises are more likely to come at the end of a protracted period of debilitation than to arise suddenly and lead to immediate death.

Medicare will only help with the acute crisis.

It is estimated that presently 50% of the population needs custodial care toward the end of their lives. Thus, you should make some plans. In discussing these issues, I have often had people respond as follows: "Oh, you are just creating a semantic issue. Yes, you are right, Medi*care* does not cover custodial care, it is Medi*caid* which covers custodial care, and Medicaid will step in where Medicare leaves off." They are both right and wrong. A difference between Medicare and Medicaid is that the former covers acute health problems and the latter covers long-term custodial health problems. But that is not the only difference. Another difference is that everyone may participate in Medicare (even those who are not in Social Security), but only the indigent—the demonstrably poor—can participate in Medicaid. As with university financial aid programs, in order to receive help, one must demonstrate financial need. In addition, as with university financial aid programs, we are likely to find ourselves on a cusp in which we are poor enough that these problems cause significant personal and financial disruption, but have just enough resources that we do not meet the criteria for *need* as the system defines it.

There *is* an exception to what has just been said: under special and specific circumstances, Medicare will pay for custodial care. Those circumstances involve hospice care. More specifically, in this context, hospice care is for patients who are terminally ill, and its purpose is to provide comfort at the patient's home during the terminal period. Specifically, hospice care requires that what is called *aggressive medicine* is not practiced on the patient except where the purpose of the measure is to alleviate pain. In order for the patient to qualify for hospice care, the attending physician must sign an affidavit indicating that the patient is terminally ill and that the prognosis is for less than six months of life. In addition, the patient must be part of an approved hospice program. If someone meets all the requirements, the benefits are surprisingly generous in light of the opposition to custodial care on the part of Medicare.

However, even under these circumstances, Medicare will not cover the entire cost. Furthermore, by invoking hospice care, the patient gives up any right to standard Medicare coverage.

Medicaid Planning

Medicaid is designed for people who are indigent and cannot care for themselves. Such people are assigned to nursing homes which provide basic custodial care and accept Medicaid payments in return. Obviously, if you really are indigent, you should look into Medicaid.

Some people become indigent paying for their long-term custodial care themselves, and after that they are picked up by Medicaid. It is not difficult to imagine that many of us who suffer long-term debilitating illnesses will be driven to indigence eventually, no matter how well we plan for our retirement. Custodial nursing care may cost over $100 each day in today's dollars without taking into account any other costs. The retirement income and savings available to us are likely to be exhausted in the face of such charges. When those resources are exhausted, Medicaid will support a person in a Medicaid facility.

Before developing the remainder of this section, I confess that I cannot write it without allowing my own moral and political biases to intrude. I recognize that my views represent a minority opinion, and I am respectfully cautious in the face of that, but I cannot discuss this topic without expressing them.

In my view, the poverty issue has brought out the worst in some people, in their accountants, lawyers, and other advisers. In order to understand what is being suggested from many quarters, I shall make a distinction between what I shall call *de facto* poverty and *de jure* poverty. The difference, obviously, is between someone who is in fact indigent and someone who is indigent by definition of legal criteria. Some people fall into both categories, and they are the people for whom Medicaid was appropriately designed. Currently, there are people who, for a price, will show affluent clients how to create a condition of *de jure* poverty without falling into *de facto* poverty. Thus, the client may gain the benefits of Medicaid without *actually* needing them. This process is called *Medicaid planning,* and I shall call the condition they wish to create *simpliciter de jure* poverty.

There is a small but growing do-it-yourself literature on the topic of medicaid planning, and advisers are ready to teach you the tricks. Both the literature and the advisers show people how to hide their assets and declare themselves to be indigent when they are not. For example, the regulations have created a loophole designed to enable the healthy spouse to continue living in a commonly owned house after the spouse needing long-term care has gone to the nursing home. That loophole was obviously created for humane reasons. It would seem doubly punitive to exhaust the assets of the spouse in need of care so thoroughly that the jointly held house would have to be sold to pay for long-term care, requiring the healthy spouse to move into unfamiliar and unpleasant housing. One form of advice from the Medicaid planners is to load a considerable amount of one's assets into the house, thus shielding it from the *de jure* definition of poverty. One has the image of one spouse, supposedly indigent, gaining the advantage of Medicaid while the other spouse lives in an opulent home and drives to visit the ill spouse in a new luxury car (which is, also, exempted from many *de jure* poverty calculations). Once having built the value of the house substantially, the healthy spouse might gain some income from it by, for example, a reverse annuity mortgage (see chapter 5). There are many other devices, and I now hear another phrase, "Medicaid trusts," which are obviously trusts designed to shield assets from the Medicaid need calculations and gain governmental support for people who are not *de facto* indigent. I shall not go on with descriptions because after a while, it may sound like I am arguing that people should not destroy parts of the library collection while describing in detail how it can be done. If you have different scruples than I about these things, there are both books and advisers available.

In a sense, each of the devices for Medicaid planning, which predate Medicaid itself, are perfectly reasonable ways for preparing for the final period of your life. They have been cleverly adjusted to take advantage of Medicaid opportunities and to open up an industry of Medicaid planning which threatens to give planning a bad name.

My political concerns on this topic are related to my moral concerns. I believe there is a national need for adequate long-term custodial care and that something should be done. I am concerned that converting Medicaid from a system designed for those who suffer from both *de facto* and *de jure* poverty to a system for *simpliciter de jure* poverty will diminish the concern for this topic. My concern proceeds along two lines. Under the assumption that the current costs of Medicaid are the costs for truly impoverished people, it is easy politically to scare us away from extending Medicaid to people who are poor but not indigent. Second, allowing these egregious misuses of the system diminishes the incentive for the private sector to respond with insurance, lifetime care communities, or other creative alternatives. For example, if people believe that by some clever maneuvering they can avoid the costs of long-term custodial care and still gain the benefits, they may not be as inclined to purchase long-term care insurance. If, however, the problems which created the loopholes were dealt with creatively, perhaps the pool of insurable people who saw the need for insurance would grow, so that the costs would drop and there would be a prospect for a successful business there. In my experience, as often as not, the driving force behind these efforts to manipulate the Medicaid system is not the patient or his or her spouse, but the next generation of prospective heirs, who hate to think their inheritance might be spent on custodial care when the government will pay for it.

If there is more passion than usual in what I have said about Medicaid planning, I am not embarrassed. Most of this maneuvering reminds me of the manipulations some families accomplish in order to establish need in their children's financial aid applications. In that case, too, there is a growing list of advisers ready to help. The aim is to put the family in *sim-pliciter de jure* poverty, so that the university will give their child financial aid, and between the government and those who pay full tuition, someone else will pay for a significant part of their child's education. Unless you have worked closely with a financial aid office, you cannot imagine the extremes to which some people will go in order to avoid their responsibilities.

Forms of financial aid are an important aspect of university life. They are designed for people who genuinely need help. As a former senior administrator, I have solicited and received gifts for scholarship funds from people with the highest and most admirable motives—people who wanted to give a chance to deserving students who had worked hard but could not afford university tuition. At the same time, I have seen people hide their assets—people I knew well enough to know that they were in better shape financially than any of us—yet they had manipulated the system to get financial aid for their children, while we, whose income is an easily traceable salary, paid the full freight for our children. The fact that as financial aid administrators, we ultimately turned to requesting a 1040 from each financial aid applicant was testimony to our inability to trust our clientele.

I was once called upon by a lawyer representing a wealthy alumnus. The lawyer said that he had a proposal to make, and he claimed that his research revealed what he would suggest was perfectly legitimate. His client's eldest child had just been admitted to the college, and everyone hoped the two other children would follow in their sibling's footsteps. His client was prepared to *contribute* enough money to the college's endowment so that the income would generate enough to defray the cost of one year's tuition, room, and board. The only proviso was that we would agree that his client's children would have the first use of the income. Of course, he reassured me that there would be no unusual pressure on the college to admit the other two children, but they were even smarter than their eldest sibling. (A few reasonable assumptions and a little arithmetic could show that the father might make money on the procedure.) The lawyer also wanted to know if there was a way I could discover that the children could in addition be recipients of basic opportunity grants and supplementary education opportunity grants from the federal government, so that the father's contribution would not have to be so large. After a few days' courteous pause for "due consideration," we declined the opportunity.

The reason for all the maneuvering with Medicaid planning is that there is a real need for some protection from the substantial yet unpredictable expenses of long-term custodial care. In general, the solutions offered have not been adequate. Two alternatives exist, which are discussed next. The first is private insurance to cover long-term custodial care.

Insurance for Long-Term Custodial Care

From a market perspective, the need for long-term custodial care insurance exists, and the need, to use a medical term, is acute. The middle class is simply not covered for long-term custodial care. There are some insurance plans, and there will probably be more in the future. As with all insurance, you should be sure to read the policy information carefully and go over it, where advisable, with an objective professional. The policies are age-related, so premiums will rise with your age. The policies may have provisions for waiting periods designed to prevent you from putting off purchasing them until you actually need them.

It is also wise to investigate the possibility of planning to pay directly for your care rather than using insurance. While that may be expensive, you *may* be able to cover it and save the cost of the premiums, which can be expensive. Just because insurance is available does not mean that it should be purchased. Recognizing that 50% of the population will probably need some long-term care, we conclude, then, that 50% will not. Abstractly, you have as much chance of falling in one group as in the other, though improved medical services mean that the odds are increasing that you will need the care. In addition, it is important to realize that most people who enter nursing homes do not spend many years there. Studies indicate that the majority of people require such care for less than a year before they die.

The health problems confronted by such people are, by and large, associated with imminent death. Nevertheless, a minority of people do experience long-term, lingering illnesses for several years before they die. That possibility does suggest an insurance approach, but one which would begin coverage after a period of time during which the insured paid for his or her care directly. For long-term care, we should seek just the opposite protection from that sought for acute care. We should look for coverage in case of demonstrably long-term illnesses. The demonstration would be reasonably easy to assess: the insured would have already paid for custodial care before turning to the long-term care insurance. Such provisions would minimize the small claims which are so expensive for insurance companies to process. They would also have insurance do what it should do: use a pooling process to absorb losses which individuals cannot absorb. I do not know of any long-term care custodial insurance which is structured in this way, so someone in immediate need may not find it. However, the societal need is so clear that I believe it will be supplied sometime soon.

People also try to arrange for long-term custodial care in their homes. Many psychological reasons support that effort, and while some long-term custodial care insurance policies allow it, in general, its advisability is related not so much to finances as to personal preference.

Part of your retirement planning should include provisions for both acute medical care and long-term custodial medical care. Thus far, I have been disappointed with the policies I have examined. Each one has provisions constraining payout, and each has a number of areas in which judgments will have to be made. Unfortunately, those judgments will be made by adjusters hired by the insurance company, whose interest is in favor of less coverage. You will not be in much of a position, either mentally or physically, to protest vigorously the adjuster's findings. TIAA has recently announced a "LongTerm Care" insurance program. It is well worth careful examination, though it, too, has severely restrictive provisions for coverage. For example, the plan literature says that it will not pay for care provided in an institution licensed to care primarily for patients with mental illnesses. In addition, TIAA's plan, like others I have examined, has provisions for starting coverage only after a subset of what are called Adult Daily Living Activities cannot be performed by the subject. Those activities often include bathing, eating, dressing, going to the toilet, moving from a bed to a chair, and maintaining continence. Benefits from the insurance may depend on your being unable to accomplish three of those activities. Suppose, then, you are in the following situation:

1. You cannot prepare your own meals, clean the dishes, or operate the dishwasher safely, but you can eat meals already prepared.
2. You cannot *safely* use a bathtub, but you can sponge bathe at the basin.
3. You can dress yourself, but you cannot clean your clothes, because you cannot operate a washing machine.
4. You can get out of bed.
5. You can get to the toilet, but you are incontinent.
6. No rational person would want you living at home alone.

The insurance for which you have paid substantial premiums for many years may not cover you by virtue of an adjuster's defensible reading of the policy. The prospect of debates with insurance adjusters in the last years of your life may lead you to consider lifetime care communities.

Lifetime Care Communities

In a sense, lifetime care communities try to create the best of all worlds. They are communities—physical communities—

which provide for progressive health care as the residents become older. They are total community operations, reminiscent of the socialist experiments in the United States and England during the early nineteenth century.

In general, you must be at least sixty years old to join one of these communities. The concept of the community is that people join it by first paying a substantial entrance fee. The fees vary widely, largely because they are handled differently. When the communities were first created, they typically retained the fee, but there were so many objections to that procedure that some communities have recently made arrangements to return a portion of the fee at the end, which means it will go into your estate. While the return of the fee may appeal to you, I have never seen a proposal for such a return which would make it an attractive investment, and in a pure investment sense, you pay for the privilege. Once again, you can see why I suggested that you should be cautious about committing yourself early or extensively to annuities. If you should decide that a lifetime care community is the best alternative, you may need to take a lump sum from your retirement savings to pay the entrance fee.

Typically, the entrance fee functions as the purchase price for the first small house or condominium in which you will live. In addition to the entrance fee, there will be regular monthly fees which may also vary, depending upon the community and the services used (for example, custodial services for cleaning your living space, meals, services of attending medical staff regularly or periodically, etc.) In addition, all the communities I have investigated require residents to pay for the equivalent of one meal a day for their dining facilities. Monthly fees may be around $1,000 per month per person, so the decision to join such a community is not to be taken lightly.

In return, once you join such a community, your basic needs are satisfied for the remainder of your life. Generally, you move into different facilities as your medical needs demand. Thus, you might start living independently in a separate house, a condominium, a cooperative, or an apartment. If you require increased assistance as you grow older, you will move into facilities where those needs can be accommodated. As your custodial needs change, there should be some provision for you in the different facilities. Your acute medical needs will still be met in the customary ways, and you will have to continue with acute care medical insurance. Your long-term custodial care should be provided by the community no matter how extensive. In short, you should have no reason for concern about your basic needs for the remainder of your life.

For parents who want to be sure they are never a burden to their children, lifetime care communities are an ultimate way to fulfill that goal. As long as your health permits, of course, you will have considerable mobility. Assuming that the law allows, there is no reason that you cannot keep your own car, and if you want to go someplace on your own, you are free to do so. Obviously, if you wish to take a trip someplace, that is for you to decide (assuming you can afford it after taking into account your expenses in the community). You should be as free as a member of the community as you were before you joined. Another advantage of this situation is that it is a way to ease into the final stages before your death. The dislocations and lurching which can be so traumatic for people as they pass through each stage are largely eliminated because there is an orderly progression from one stage to another.

As you become older and more infirm, you will be moved from one level of care to the next in the retirement community you have chosen. You will not have to be persuaded against your will, and for some period of time, your previous residence should be kept available for you. In the end, assuming death comes gradually rather than as a result of a sudden illness or accident, you will be in what is in essence a hospice, where the primary goal is to make you comfortable and give you as much quality of life as your body will allow in the remaining years of your life. Assuming you have found the community compatible, we can hope you will feel comfortable in the various stages. Presumably, you will die in the community, but you will die in the company of friends and supportive people you know rather than as a stranger in a nursing home or hospital.

In addition, there is the great benefit of knowing you are safe, cared for, and watched over. If people in the community do not hear from you for a while, they are likely to pay a visit and see how you are doing. If they find something wrong, they will take appropriate action. The community itself should be well guarded and protected, so you will not have to worry about burglaries and physical harm. (Your loved ones will not have to worry about you in that regard either.)

There are some disadvantages to this arrangement. First, some will find it suffocating and unpleasant. You may be expected to participate in the social activities arranged for community residents. Of course, you probably do not *have to* participate, but there may be informal pressures to do so, and those who seek peace and quiet on their own may feel ostracized from the others in the community. As academics, we need to remember that we are not like other people. Many of us will resist such regimentation almost viscerally. We have been taught to be critical, and it is unlikely that we shall turn that off in our dotage. Individual faculty members should think about how content they may be in such a setting.

A commitment to a lifetime care community is a major step. In some cases, it is impossible to recover the entrance fee once it has been paid, and even when the fee can be recovered, there is customarily a steep price to pay. The most desirable communities often have a waiting list for new residents. There is typically little penalty for putting your name on the waiting list and withdrawing, and if you are interested, it may be wise to submit your name. Often, the lists are kept on a rotating basis, so that when a suitable opening is available, if you are not ready, your name goes to the bottom of the list.

You cannot wait too long for a commitment of this nature, however. Lifetime care communities have custodial care facilities, but they do not allow themselves to become nursing homes. Usually, you will be refused entrance if you cannot live independently when you enter. Thus, you cannot wait until you are unable to care for yourself. That will be too late, and you will have to go directly to a nursing home.

Once again, it is important for you and your objective advisers to review all documents and commitments you may be making. Do not be afraid to request changes in the arrangements. Be sure any special arrangements which are important to you are in writing. You should also examine carefully the financial health of the community. You do not want to get into such a community only to have it file for bankruptcy just as you need the custodial services. If you are not confident of your own ability to examine its financial health, you might do the primary work and analysis yourself and then ask a professional financial planner to review the material for you. You should have little interest in any community which is not willing to reveal as much information in as much detail as you wish.

There is an accreditation association for lifetime care communities: The American Association of Homes for the Aging, 1129 20th Street, NW, Washington, DC 20036. As with colleges and universities, the accreditation process is voluntary. As of the writing of this book, there were only seventy duly accredited lifetime care communities in the United States. Gerontologists have estimated that there are perhaps more than ten times that number which are unaccredited. If you are interested in further research on lifetime care communities, you might start with the accredited ones. The association will send you a list of them. It is very important to read and understand all documentation and to review it with objective advisers. Some operations pretend to be total care communities when they are not, and others appear to be a bargain but keep extra charges in small print. It does not follow that just because one operation is more expensive than another, it is better. At the same time, it does not follow that just because some organization appears to charge less than another, it is a bargain. Careful analysis is important because of the long-term and all-inclusive nature of the commitment.

In the past few years, some colleges and universities have gone into the lifetime care community business. Given their successes with other community operations, it makes sense for them to extend their activities in these directions. It certainly would make sense for you to examine these possibilities, because you might enjoy the advantages of living near a campus. Some cases I have examined offer opportunities for members of the community to interact with students, to take classes, and even to teach classes with the full-time faculty. All of that may be attractive to you, and it would be worth investigating if you are interested in the general concept of lifetime care communities.

8

Late Retirement Planning
and Death

Preparation for Death

Death is the final irreversible event in our experience. I promised at the outset of this book that I would not patronize readers by using euphemisms to avoid obvious facts. The sections on long-term medical care were written with the hope that we could retain the dignity of our life as it comes to its conclusion. This chapter deals directly with that final period. The hope is that by planning we can provide for the disposition of our property in a way which reflects positively on our lives and satisfies our own desires and interests. My presumption is that we want to cause a minimum of disruption in the lives of those who remain living. Planning for the late retirement years phases naturally into estate planning, though that term may seem somewhat presumptuous to many people.

The changes in mandatory retirement, Social Security, and TIAA-CREF provisions have been symptoms of deeper changes in our careers and lives in retirement. All of the changes I have discussed have given us more control and flexibility for managing our lives. Our predecessors had to retire by sixty-five or seventy and after choosing from the annuity alternatives offered by TIAA-CREF, they retired with very limited further control or flexibility with regard to the financial aspects of the remainder of their lives. Under the new circumstances, you have more opportunities, and it makes sense to make explicit decisions about what happens to your possessions and property after you die. In addition, it is possible that, having taken some measure of control, you will die with an estate for which planning makes sense. If you have not automatically adopted an annuity approach, and if you have followed some of the advice offered here for managing your retirement savings as well as medical insurance protection, you can be optimistic about having some assets in your estate when you die. It is important, then, to make provisions for the distribution of those assets.

Wills

As I indicated earlier, I cannot think of any good reasons not to have a will, and I can think of many for having one. But before you consider what may be your final will, think carefully about what you want to accomplish. In a sense, the best legacy you can give to those who follow you is a legacy of clarity. Do not assume that everyone knows what you want. Equally destructive is the assumption that you do not really care. The events which follow the disposition of property after someone's death are a fit subject for a considerable body of literature, and not all of it is fiction.

If you have a favorite stamp collection and one of your children is the only person who has shown a serious interest in it, do not assume that your estate executrix or executor will know it should go to that child. Say explicitly what you want done. You can always change your mind before you die, but the courts will not accept your testimony after you have died, through whatever medium. You will be gone, so you should take the responsibility for these decisions and not leave them to those who follow. Let people get mad at you because you left something to someone who was "obviously" the wrong person. They may complain, but in the end they will have to respect your wishes.

Do not think some topics are too specific to matter. The

more you specify, the easier it will be to execute your wishes with the least controversy. For example, what do you want done with your old manuscripts, and what should happen to former student dissertations? (I say toss them, but you may not feel the same way). At the same time, be careful about inflicting obligations on people who follow you. It may be no favor if you "give" your library to someone with the stipulation that it should be kept intact. Any potential recipient *does* have the right to refuse an inheritance, but the decision may be psychologically difficult. You should have an "all other" category, too, so it will be clear that what is not designated goes to someone or someplace.

Once you are clear about what you wish to accomplish, you are ready to begin to revise your will as a first pass. There are kits for doing this, and there is software if you like using computers. It is not difficult, however, and it can be done as a first pass reasonably easily. Your will should specify how your final expenses (funeral expenses, burial expenses, etc.) are to be paid.

In specifying sums of money to be given to persons, be careful to make your intentions clear. For example, if you designate a particular sum of money, you may preclude having someone else receive the bulk of your estate as you intended. Suppose, for example, when you drew up your will, you had $500,000 in cash and other assets of little significance. Suppose you decided that you wanted your favorite charity to receive half your estate, which you designated as $250,000, and your child to receive the remainder, which at the time you signed your will would mean at least $250,000. Then, suppose you had an extended illness which depleted your estate to the extent that by the time of your death, there was only $250,000 in the estate along with other assets of little significance. The charity would probably receive $250,000, and your child would receive the assets of little significance because your will set the first amount in dollar terms. Perhaps you should have said that you wanted your child and the charity each to get one-half without specifying dollar amounts. On the other hand, if you were really most committed to your child receiving at least $250,000, you should have said so. The will must be probated as it reads and not as someone may think you probably intended. You and your advisers should be alert for unintended consequences, but the primary responsibility must fall on your shoulders, because only you can know what you intend.

You will need to name an executrix or executor for your will. Think about that designation carefully, and if it is a friend or relative, be sure to make some provision for reimbursement. The executrix or executor is your representative after your death in the matter of the distribution of your assets. She or he is also responsible for the administration of your estate and the management of its assets until they are distributed. She or he is also responsible for insuring that appropriate federal estate taxes and state death taxes are paid. Fulfilling the conditions of a will is not easy even in the best of circumstances. Some people suggest designating an organization as executor, since organizations can be presumed to exist in perpetuity. You may have some difficulty with that, because the minimum fee could amount to a large portion of your estate. If you decide to designate an organization, be sure you examine its fee schedule. You should ask, also, to be put on a regular mailing list to inform you of any changes in fees. You could name the law firm of the person who drew up your will with a named preference for that person, if that makes sense to you. You could name your financial planner or his or her successor or partner, if that seems appropriate. Think about the designation carefully and be sure to discuss it with whomever is named. It is not an impossible task for a reasonably intelligent person. You and the person should expect to need the services of a lawyer during the settlement of the estate.

If you select an individual, you will not be doing that person any favors, though I find that most people are willing to do it as a favor to a friend. Be sure to make clear in the will that the executrix or executor is to call upon whatever help she or he thinks is needed in carrying out the duties. If you have any fears that the person might use that opportunity to take too much from your estate in the guise of support services, you have selected the wrong person. It is true that heirs may always object to such charges. In the extreme, they may even sue. However, the ideal is to have someone whose integrity is respected by all parties and who will be sure the specifications of your will are carried out. You should consider naming a contingent executrix or executor in case the first designated one either cannot or will not fulfill the responsibilities when the time comes. In these days of unstable financial institutions and law firms, I suggest a contingent executrix or executor even if the primary one is an organization. While corporate charters presume perpetuity, that does not guarantee it. You need to discuss your will with the first-named and the contingent designees. Do not avoid that responsibility, and be prepared to go through the will in detail to be sure they know what you are doing.

When you have completed a first draft of your will, you may want to discuss it with your financial planner and then go through it carefully with your lawyer. The lawyer should be familiar with the federal laws and the laws of your state. Your financial planner and your lawyer may make some suggestions for changes. You should consider those suggestions carefully and ask for an analysis of their implications. However, remember that this is *your* will, not theirs. Be sure you accomplish what you want in the process. I suggest that you should not try to write the official will yourself; that is the lawyer's job. However, by doing the initial work, you will have reduced the nonlegal work for the lawyer, and his or her fee should be less. In addition, you will have gained the greatest benefit of your lawyer's expertise.

There is only one official copy of your will. You need to give some thought to where it is kept. The courts will only accept the original, though you may have as many copies as you wish. The reason for establishing that the original is the only official copy is that one way to retract your will is to destroy the original. Some people suggest keeping the official copy with the lawyer. That makes sense, though other people also worry about what they would do in the event that they no longer had confidence in the lawyer who drew up the will. Another natural place to think of for keeping your will is in your safe deposit box in the bank, but that *can* pose a "catch-22." The bank may not let anyone but you into your safe deposit box (because you are the one with signature authority), but you are dead! Thus, your heirs may be forced to wait until a court official is designated to do an inventory of the contents of the box, and that may be inconvenient. You might keep the official copy of your will at home. Some people worry that it could be lost in a fire or some other disaster. That is true, but another could be drawn up quickly if that were to happen. A more realistic worry might be that it will be someplace where it cannot be found. There may be other reasonable and imaginative ways to handle the problem, but you should give it some thought and carry out whatever plan makes most sense to you. Be sure to tell your executor or executrix where the official copy of the will is located.

If you are married, your spouse should have a will, also. Ideally, the two wills should be closely coordinated. In loving marriages, I suggest that the two wills should be reviewed by the same financial planners and finally created by the same lawyers. You should also have what is called a "common disaster" clause which indicates what should happen if both of you die simultaneously.

Ownership of Property

The development of your will provides another occasion on which you should review the ownership of your property. Ownership provisions are not a substitute for a will, but it is important that they are clear and coordinated with your will. As you will recall, ownership provisions take precedence over provisions of a will. It is important to review the conditions of ownership and decide whether those conditions are consistent with your intentions after your death.

Beyond that, I suggest holding some funds jointly with a trusted person. Many people suggest having a durable power of attorney prepared so someone can make decisions for you in case you are not able to do so. That is a wise suggestion, and while you are having your lawyer prepare your will, you might ask that a durable power of attorney be prepared. However, I have known occasions when an authority who had control over something the trusted friend needed to help you would not accept the use of a power of attorney. In such circumstances, the friend may, of course, have the lawyer tell the official about powers of attorney. The friend may ask to see superiors and get them to enforce powers of attorney, and so forth. However, all of us who have dealt with (public or private) bureaucracies know that when some bureaucrats are angered, they can make life difficult and miserable—just at a time when no more misery is needed. A joint bank account or a joint money market fund may be very useful, because the friend trying to help you can have access to money to get things done, at least while you wait out the bureaucrats. (I do not preclude the possibility that a spouse may be the "friend" as that is construed in the previous sentence!)

Consider, also, physical property such as automobiles. Property which is solely owned by a deceased person cannot be used legally by someone else until after so authorized by the probate process. Probate without a will can take a long time. Probate in the presence of a will should move along more quickly, but it can still take time. Thus, review ownership provisions with the assumption that you are going to die soon, and ask yourself whether what you have provided is what you want.

Estate Planning

Estate planning is a sensible, if somewhat pompous, term which should apply primarily to what has been discussed already: planning for the disposition of whatever property and possessions you leave after your death. Under some circumstances, the decisions covered will constitute all you need to do. However, those circumstances are restricted, and federal estate taxes as well as state death taxes rise so rapidly that it will be important to take them into account if your situation should demand it. I cannot discuss state taxes here beyond suggesting that they should be considered carefully. The differences among the states are significant, and in some circumstances those taxes may have a significant impact on your estate, your heirs, and your plans for distribution. With regard to federal taxes, once your estate has passed a minimum level, the taxes become significant and rise rapidly. For example, the effective marginal estate tax rate itself starts at approximately 37% and rises quickly to 55%. There is an automatic deduction and a special provision for spouses, both of which are discussed in the next paragraphs. There is also some provision for deducting some of the state's death taxes from your federal estate taxes, but that varies depending on the state.

Let us look at conditions in which you can continue to be your own primary financial planner and basically ignore the tax aspects of your estate planning. First, if your only concern is with regard to your spouse and if his or her only concern is with regard to you, current regulations include a 100% spousal deduction for all estate taxes. Thus, you may leave your spouse your entire estate, no matter what its value may be, and your spouse will receive it without any *federal* estate tax being paid. That provision is independent of the gender of the spouse. There may well be tax implications after that, but if the only concern of you and your spouse is for each other, those tax implications after the death of both of you may be irrelevant to you. I should note an exception to the 100% spousal deduction: it does not apply if the spouse receiving the inheritance is not a citizen of the United States. If you or your spouse are not citizens of the United States, you will need to seek advice from legal counsel in this special area. The sooner you receive the advice, the better. Planning ahead may help mitigate the impact of such restrictions, but if you wait until the last minute, the restrictions may be severe.

Second, there is an automatic deduction in the federal estate tax which must be paid. It may be helpful to go through the arithmetic with an imaginary example to make a few points clear. Suppose you were to die leaving an estate in cash and securities worth $600,000, and no other assets. Suppose you were not married and decided to give your entire estate to your sister. In computing the federal estate tax, your executrix or executor would see in the tax tables that for estates of between $500,000 and $750,000, the tax on the first $500,000 is $155,800 and the tax on everything over that up to $750,000 is taken at 37%. The difference between $500,000 and $600,000 is $100,000, and the tax on that is $37,000. Thus, the total federal tax bill calculated before deductions would be $192,800. However, each estate has an automatic deduction of $192,800 for its federal estate taxes. Thus, no tax would be owed. One point to be made is that even though your estate will not have to pay a federal estate tax, the tax itself must be calculated and reported. A second point allows you to see the origin of my earlier statement that the effective marginal estate rate begins at 37%. Finally, it should also be clear that once the deduction is passed, the tax rate makes a significant difference. For example, if the imaginary estate had been worth $750,000 instead of $600,000, the tax on the incremental $150,000 would be approximately $55,500, and that tax would have to be paid before the estate could be settled.

As your final estate rises above the $600,000 level and as you desire to provide for others beyond your spouse, you will have an increasing need for professional estate planning help. The entire area is so complex and subject to so much continual change that I cannot recommend that you do even your own primary estate planning. The larger your estate is than $600,000, the more you will need professional help. The consequences can be so dramatic and the area is so technical that this is no place to attempt to go it alone or to cut costs. The substitution of a few simple words which may seem synonymous to you and me can make an enormous amount of difference in the effect of the estate in terms of the taxes paid and in terms of what may be available to your heirs. The most I can do in this book is to help you ask the right questions and pursue various considerations. Consequently, I shall list some topics and strategies which may be of interest to you and which you may wish to discuss with your estate planner. In this context, it is also important that you find an estate planner whose primary concern is your interests. As in the case of financial planners, there are a number of people who call themselves estate planners but who have other interests which may conflict with yours. I would not refuse to read whatever they wished to suggest, and if I had the time, I would not refuse to talk with them. They may be able to make useful suggestions that you and your objective estate planner have not considered. However, before you make any decisions, you should be sure to discuss the whole situation with your financial planner, your estate planner and/or your lawyer. There are numerous devices and strategies which may be useful in minimizing estate taxes. I can only suggest a few on the assumption that you may want to discuss them with your advisers as they suggest an estate-planning strategy for you.

■ *Equalizing Assets* If you are married, one of the simplest things you can do is to equalize the asset distribution between you and your spouse. In that way, upon the death of each, full benefit can be taken of the $600,000 exclusion. For example, suppose you had assets of $1,200,000 and your spouse had no assets. If you were to die and leave everything to your spouse, the 100% marital deduction means that there would be no federal estate tax. However, if your spouse were to die soon thereafter, leaving the total $1,200,000 to your children, that estate would enjoy the first $600,000 exclusion and then pay federal estate taxes on the next $600,000, which would amount to about $235,000. Your children would divide $956,000. If, however, you had equalized the assets, your $600,000 could have gone to your children directly and there would be no estate tax. When your spouse died shortly thereafter, that $600,000 would have gone to the children in total so they would have received the $1,200,000 in total. Obviously, there are advantages and disadvantages to this kind of arrangement, and there are other variations, as indicated in the later discussion of trusts. The point to be reenforced, however, is that the differences can be financially substantial, and professional advice is necessary.

■ *Lifetime Gifts* The federal estate tax is a combined gift and estate tax. The purpose is to recognize that if gifts are not taxable to the recipient and if there are no provisions for taxation, they would provide a way around estate taxes entirely. Thus, the $600,000 minimum discussed earlier may be used at the time of death, or it may be used during your lifetime. If you use it during your lifetime, it will be folded into your estate for the calculation of your estate taxes. In general, it is most useful in that context as an effort to "freeze" the value of a gift which you intend to make upon your death. Suppose, for example, you were the owner of the family homestead and you intended to leave it to your children upon your death. Suppose, however, that real estate prices were rising rapidly in its real estate market. The value of the homestead for your estate tax purposes will be taken at the assessed value when it is transferred. If you were to give the homestead to your children now, the transfer *might* be made at a lower value than if it waited until your death. However, it is important to point out that the transfer of ownership must be complete. There must be an absolute and *irrevocable* transfer of legal title and of the control and use of the gift. You must have an unequivocal intention to completely eliminate any interest of your own in the property. As I understand the situation, you must be careful about any clever arrangements which would attenuate such conditions. Again, you may want to ask about such possibilities, but you should use the professionals. A second form of lifetime gifts are modest-sized gifts which you can make through your lifetime. You may make gifts of up to $10,000 annually to any other person, though this provision is often understood to be especially relevant for children. If you are married and your wife joins you in the annual gift, it may be up to $20,000. That may not seem like much, but over the years it can mount rapidly, and it moves assets out of your estate, which means that they will avoid estate taxes. Since such distributions may have an impact on your retirement and your total estate, you should discuss them with your advisers. There is a citizenship exception here, also. If your spouse is not a citizen of the United States, he or she may *not* join you to create a $20,000 gift.

∎ *2503(c) Trusts* If you wish to use your annual gift exclusion powers, but you do not wish to give the recipient control over the use of the assets, you and your advisers may consider a 2503(c) trust named—imaginatively—after the section in the code. These have been suggested especially for people with younger children or grandchildren. They wish to make the gifts for tax reasons, but they do not want the young people to have control over those sums of money. There are technical specifications which should be considered with the professionals carefully. The designation of the trustee is important. These trusts must terminate when the child turns twenty-one or upon his or her death (care must be taken so that in the event of the death of the child, the assets do not return to your estate.)

∎ *Crummey Trusts* These trusts are named after the person who took a case successfully through litigation. Like 2503(c) trusts, they are a vehicle for receiving annual lifetime gifts. They do not have to terminate when the child turns twenty-one. However, the child has the legal right to demand money from the trust. There is a trade-off in regard to those issues. It is important to recognize that, once again, the details are very important, and these trusts, as all others, should be set up by a competent and qualified attorney.

∎ *Life Insurance Trusts* In these trusts, you would create a trust which owns a life insurance policy on your life. However, you pay the premiums on the policy perhaps using your annual gift exclusion. You then have the flexibility of naming the beneficiary or beneficiaries, and that may be useful in estate planning, especially where liquidity may be an issue in regard to paying estate taxes. As with other gifts, if you are going to use this form of trust for tax purposes, you must *really* give up any interest in the policy—interest in regard to changes in beneficiaries, the right to cancel the policy or reassign it, and so on. These strategies are likely to work only when you have created what is called an *irrevocable trust.* If the trust is revocable (i.e., you can reverse the process at will) then the IRS is likely to refuse to accept the arrangement, and your efforts at tax avoidance will have gone for naught.

There is a variation of the standard life insurance trust which may be of interest in specific circumstances. It is sometimes called a "second-to-die" life insurance trust. It may be particularly appropriate where you are responsible for young children even though you are moving into retirement. Suppose, for example, in a second marriage, the faculty member is substantially older than the nonfaculty spouse, and they have young children. Suppose, in addition, that the nonfaculty spouse works elsewhere in an organization with a defined-benefit retirement program which does not pay a death benefit. The couple might plan that if either were to die, the other spouse would have enough resources to take care of the children. However, they might be concerned that if both of them were to die while the children are still young, the children's guardians would need substantial resources to care for the children and their education. In those circumstances, the couple might consider a life insurance trust which owns a life insurance policy that pays only on the death of *both* of them. That life insurance is likely to be considerably less expensive than life insurance on one of them, yet it may cover the contingency which concerns them while keeping the funds in trust so that immature children do not have access to them. In the matter of all trusts, including life insurance trusts, care is necessary. You should use your fee-only financial planner, who may be able to find you life insurance which is less expensive because it does not pay sales commissions. You should also be sure that the trust is set up by a competent attorney. Your life insurance agent may be a nice person, but, even if he or she is called a financial planner, using such people to avoid an attorney may prove to be harmful to your heirs.

■ *By-Pass Trust* If you have over $600,000 and you want to reduce the estate taxes on assets which may be distributed after your death, you may want to ask your estate planner about the possibility of a by-pass trust. Fundamentally, the trust is constructed so that at your death it receives $600,000 of your assets (the amount derived as above). It may hold that amount in trust and allow someone, such as your spouse, to receive the income. Upon your spouse's death, the assets are given to whomever you designate. It is important to recognize that this means your spouse will not have access to the principal; thus, it restricts his or her financial flexibility. Allowing for that constraint, however, it may mean that your flexibility for planning without worrying much about tax implications rises to a joint estate for you and your spouse of $1,200,000.

■ *Qualified Terminable Interest Property Trust (Q-TIP Trust)* This is a variation on the standard by-pass trust which gives *you* more control over the designation of who is to receive the principal after the second death. Some have found this useful in the case of second marriages and children from the first marriage or in the case of husbands who fear they will predecease their wives, who may then remarry and add others to the beneficiaries of the trust.

■ *Charitable Remainder Trusts* The development office in your university can probably give you information about these trusts. The trust is set up by a charitable institution. You give the trust an amount of money. Depending upon your arrangements with the charity, the trust in turn gives you and a named beneficiary an annual income for life. By IRS regulations, that income may not be less than 5% of the amount of the money initially given to the trust if it is to qualify. Your estate should be allowed to claim a deduction equivalent to the value of the assets given to the charity's trust. That is a way to reduce the asset value of your estate and still get some income from your money. Obviously, a commitment of this nature should be reviewed with your financial planner. I would also recommend review with your attorney to be sure she or he is satisfied that the trust meets IRS regulations.

■ *Charitable Remainder Unitrusts* Once again, your university development office should have literature on these trusts. In this case, you may be able to gain some advantage from the compounding of the amoung you have given to the charity's trust account. Instead of entirely comingling your money with other monies, the trust treats your investment in a way analogous to an investment in a mutual fund, maintaining an analogy to the net asset value. The income then paid to you must be no less than 5% of the net asset value of your fund (where that value is reviewed annually). There may be two additional provisions: (1) if the actual income received by the trust and attributed to your fund falls below what 5% would have been, the trust may pay you that lesser amount; (2) if the actual income received by the trust and attributed to your fund is greater than what 5% would have been, and if you have already received a reduced distribution in accordance with (1) previously, the trust must make up the difference to the extent the extra income allows. Once again, I do not suggest that anyone try to follow these paths alone. My purpose for mentioning them is to make you aware of the possibility of alternatives so you can ask appropriate questions of the professionals. Even though I spent a considerable amount of my life discussing charitable remainder trusts with prospective donors, I always suggested—indeed, insisted—that they be sure to be guided by objective professional financial and legal advisors. If you find yourself in a position to take advantage of these provisions, I suggest no less to you.

■ *Living Trusts* As far as I can determine, living trusts do not offer any tax advantages. They are meant to be revocable trusts. You may even serve as trustee. The trust receives some or all of your assets, and they are administered through the trust during your life or until you dissolve it, which you may do for whatever reasons you deem sufficient. Upon your death, the trust may be continued in existence to make proceeds available as you have designated. That means that the proceeds pass outside your will, so they do not have to go through probate. (However, they are still part of your estate, so estate taxes will have to be calculated and paid where appropriate.) Since the trust is usually revocable only by you, once you die it becomes essentially irrevocable (though depending upon the conditions you have specified, it may distribute all its assets and then be dissolved.) Some people suggest that a living trust may do away with the need for a will, but I disagree. I think you still need a will, though the presence of a living trust may make your will more simple. If the purpose of attempting to avoid a will is to avoid paying an attorney, I do not think a living trust is appropriate because, in my view, you should have an attorney draw up the provisions for a living trust.

One announced advantage of a living trust is that it can keep secret the provisions you make for distribution of your assets after your death. After your death, a will is probated, and it becomes a public document which anyone may examine. If that potential public knowledge concerns you, a living trust is a way to avoid it. The fact of the trust will be public knowledge, but the details of the trust will not be public. Another advantage of a living trust may be that monies can start to flow to your beneficiaries immediately after your death, they do not have to wait for the probate process. In addition, living trusts make it somewhat more difficult for heirs who feel left out to find room for legal action. In the first place, they have no automatic right to know the provisions of the trust. In the second place, it is much more difficult to get the courts to overthrow the provisions of a trust than of a will. (Though, it should be pointed out that courts in general are very reluctant to overturn provisions of a will if those provisions are clear and not in violation of the law, so we are talking about degrees of improbability here.) The major disadvantages of a living trust are expense, cumbersomeness, a greater potential for miscommunication, and the fact that it may not include a significant portion of your estate. It may be more expensive to set up and administer a living trust than to set up a will. If you have put your savings in a rollover IRA, they may not be included in your living trust. IRAs are considered trusts already, so they cannot be included in other trusts.

In sum, if you have an estate which rises above the minimum amounts indicated and if you wish to do something other than leave your entire estate to your spouse and vice-versa, you will need to consider using an estate planner. The illustrations I have given above are not intended to be guides to action. They are only intended to suggest elements you might explore with your estate planner as you try to arrange for the distribution of your assets in the way which makes most sense to you. There are complications within complications in this area. For dual-income couples, where a spouse's estate may be based on some source other than a salary from an academic institution, there may be even greater complications.

However, I can make one final recommendation. Make sure you try to achieve *your* goals. I have seen cases in which people's goals were warped by their advisers in order to save taxes. The economics of the estate-planning field are such that estate planners justify their sometimes considerable fees because of the taxes they are able to save clients. Thus, some estate planners are more focused on tax-avoidance strategies than on strategies designed to achieve their clients' objectives. In my view, your objectives should have priority; saving estate taxes and death taxes should be secondary.

Living Wills

Living wills are not analogous to living trusts. Living wills indicate to people who may be responsible for the final days or hours of your life what kind of medical care you wish to have during that time. After you can no longer make decisions about your medical care, the responsibilities will fall to other people. A living will attempts to help those people decide the level of medical effort you want made. Suppose, for example, that essentially all quality of life for you has gone, and there is virtually no medically reasonable hope that it might return. A living will may guide those who must make decisions about further treatment. Some people want all and every medically possible action to be taken. Others may wish to be made comfortable as they wait for the inevitable. These are all emotionally and morally complex and difficult questions. The living will can help those who will assume responsibility for you decide how they should act and how they should instruct medical people to act. A host of questions in medical ethics arise here, including the determination of when you are being medically treated with reasonable hope of recovery and restoration and when you are merely a recipient of continuing medical experimentation—and whether you would want that.

Some states do not recognize the validity of living wills, and it is not clear how they will be treated in our adversarial legal environment when the inevitable suits are brought forward. Nevertheless, many people have advocated their use as a form of clear instruction and as a form of strengthening the resolve of people who are responsible for the care of dying patients. You may want to determine what your state allows, and you may want to decide whether you should execute such a living will. If you decide to do so, you should consider involving a lawyer, so that the document can conform as closely as possible to the particular state laws and any court precedents.

You may wish to designate someone to act in your place as medical decisions are made. Obviously, it should be a person who knows you well and can speak authoritatively about what you would want. Equally obviously, it should be someone in whom you have complete trust and faith. You will need to have some discussions with that person, and I suggest that you should be quick to release him or her from that responsibility if it becomes burdensome.

Conclusion

As we come to the end of this book, it may be useful to recall its founding principles. Recognizing the changes which have taken place in the conditions of retirement for academics, I wanted to present information and advice which would help people to take control of their lives. I believe the means of that control lies in planning. The very nature of our retirement systems requires that some serious planning for retirement be part of our lives from the start of our careers. I have suggested areas in which we could function as our own primary financial planners with occasional recourse to professional financial planners. I know of no way in which we can realistically afford to turn our backs on these responsibilities or to turn them over entirely to advisers. I have tried to suggest that in general the technical areas are not so complex that with some effort you will not be able to deal with the issues effectively and creatively. The notable exception is for those people who will have substantial estates and consequent estate planning. I could find no way to simplify that world so that it would be realistic to think that we could be our own primary estate planners. I wish it were not so, but I do not see any alternative. Having said that, however, I would hasten to add that for those academics whose estates are not so substantial (i.e., less than $600,000), the problems are not so complicated, and it is reasonable to maintain a position of personal involvement and direction.

I have avoided providing any hard prescriptions because I am so completely aware of the special circumstances of each person. I am reminded of the time when, in 1973, I became director of a project designed to make the planning processes for colleges more rational. The project was supported by the Exxon Education Foundation and involved some fairly sophisticated computer work. After we had moved one system into a testing stage, I suggested to a faculty member who was working with me that we should examine a normal department and pass its data through the system to see how the system worked.

That seemed sensible enough until we began to try to select a department, whereupon we came to realize that there was no normal department and that the system had to be prepared to include the considerable variations and special characteristics of each department. I suspect that if we were to attempt to create a rigid retirement system for academics, we would come to a similar conclusion. That recognition is at the base of my objection to the former system. It tried to cast everyone into a few very limited molds. That system is gone now, but its end does not imply that intellectual anarchy is the only alternative. Generalizations may be made, even though they will be appropriately violated in special instances. Thus, I have believed the most I could do would be to suggest some generalizations, some rules of thumb, some rebuttable assumptions, some guiding principles, and expect that each individual will establish an appropriate approach. I believed that procedure should give people the greatest realistic control over their own lives. That has been my objective; others must now decide how well it has been accomplished.

□

Appendix
Notes
Index

Appendix: Personal Investment Management

Introduction: Managing Mutual Funds

This appendix has been included because in a number of places I have suggested that you may wish to do your own investment managing. I have suggested that except in unusual cases, we should probably not attempt to buy stocks, bonds, options, and so forth directly and that if we wish to be more active in the management of our investments, in general, we should do so through the intermediary of mutual funds. In that way, we can gain the advantage of additional diversification so that our entire retirement savings will not be with one financial organization.

Since it is clear that some people will find that such involvement pushes them further over on the spectrum toward connectedness than they would like, I did not presume in the body of the book that everyone would decide to manage their own investments. Thus, I decided to put this presentation in an appendix where those who were interested could find it, and those who were not could ignore it. I have tried to make the process of personal investment management accessible to people who do not wish to be experts, so I would suggest that even those who do not plan to take charge of the investment management of their retirement savings might review the material in this appendix. You may also find it useful in making other investment decisions, such as those for IRAs and SRAs.

The appendix follows a simple strategy: first it presents a classification of the different types of mutual funds in preparation for choosing the ones most appropriate for your needs. After that, it develops a rational method for systematically selecting the appropriate funds.

I have already discussed the basic concepts of mutual funds in chapter 4, so I shall not repeat that information here. I assume that most of those who decide to manage their retirement savings more directly will do so through the use of what are called *open-end* mutual funds, so the bulk of this appendix is devoted to an exploration of them and of ways to narrow choices down to a manageable number. If you have funds in TIAA-CREF, you are already effectively using mutual fund principles. You now have the opportunity to diversify the placement of your savings and to have a program which reflects more closely your particular needs and interests.

Many people may hesitate to take the plunge into managing their own investments because there are many mutual funds and no clear way to decide in which ones you should invest. Open-end mutual funds are numerous, but I think there are some principles—rules-of-thumb—which can be used to narrow the list so that you can concentrate on a manageable number. In considering the number of mutual funds, it may help if you recognize that there are approximately as many open-end mutual funds as there are colleges and universities in the United States (just over three thousand). In the abstract, the process of choosing a mutual fund is not much different from that which prospective college students have to go through: progressively narrowing the list to an appropriate few and then making a choice. Students who do a good job of narrowing the list, will conclude with a small number of colleges, all of which would be appropriate. From that small number, they make their ultimate choice. That is the basic strategy I advocate here: progressive narrowing on rational bases and then making final choices from a manageable few. Since the principles for selecting mutual funds will vary somewhat in accordance with the type of mutual fund, the first task is to identify the different kinds of funds.

A Classification of Open-End Mutual Funds

As indicated previously, open-end mutual funds must construct a valuation of their holdings on a daily basis. That valuation is called the net asset value (NAV). It is established by taking the total value of all the individual financial instruments (for example, the closing prices of stocks) and dividing it by the number of mutual fund shares outstanding. The NAV is needed so the fund can know how much to charge for new shares and how much to pay when a customer wishes to sell shares. Most rules in the financial markets have exceptions, and this one also has an exception in regard to what are called money market mutual funds. In those funds, the fund is managed in such a way that the value of the shares is maintained at close to $1.00 per share. The purpose of that arrangement is to insure that an investor in a money market fund can get in and out quickly without losing the value of the underlying principal. There will be more discussion of money market funds later.

In purchasing shares in an open-end mutual fund, the new share-owner is, in effect, purchasing a small proportional interest in all the investments held by the mutual fund. If you wish to purchase shares, the fund will sell them to you at the NAV per share plus commission, if any. The fund exchanges your money for the appropriate amount of shares, including, typically, a fractional number of shares, so that the numbers work out. If at a later time, you wish to sell all or part of your holdings in the fund, the fund will calculate those holdings at the current NAV minus a redemption fee, if any. The funds are called *open-end* because they can have as many shareholders as wish to join. When a fund becomes popular, it issues more shares.

There is a downside to the open-end feature. If many people wish to redeem their shares at the same time, and if the fund does not have enough in cash to cover the redemptions, the portfolio manager will be obliged to sell some of the fund's securities in order to raise the required cash. Since that may come at a time when the market is out of favor in general, holdings may be sold at prices which the managers of the fund do not think are attractive. Contrariwise (as Alice said), if large amounts of cash start to flow into a fund, it may be difficult for the managers to invest it in accordance with their objectives. Suppose, for example, some people started an open-end fund because they were good at analyzing small companies and identifying managements which would do unusually well. Money might start flowing in faster than the portfolio managers could find attractive special situations. Thus, the open-end nature of these funds cuts both ways. At the same time, they have become very popular, especially for the small and mid-sized investor, because they provide a way for investors to gain instant diversification.

It is estimated that two-thirds of the investments in the stock and bond markets are done through funds and other institutional investors, not by individuals. There is a large variety of mutual funds, and while you may not be able to invest in all of them because of university policies, it is wise to understand the different possibilities before focusing on particular areas and funds which may be of interest.

There is no universally accepted way of classifying open-end mutual funds. I am suggesting a system which has proven useful and which highlights funds which may be of special interest to us. Any substantial portfolio would probably include representatives of the first three categories.

Money Market Funds

The primary purposes of money market funds are twofold: (1) to give investors a place to put their money for short periods of time and yet have it earn some interest and (2) to give investors a safe haven for their money when they foresee serious troubles ahead. The principal of the investment is usually secure; the interest rate will vary, and of course there is no assurance that money in a money market fund will be able to keep up with inflation. Seen in a rather simplistic way, money market funds have taken the place of savings accounts; their return is usually better, and the principal is reasonably secure in a large fund.

If your daily newspaper carries fairly complete financial information, it will probably have a separate listing of money market funds each Thursday. Their NAV will not be listed because, as indicated earlier, they convert your investment into shares which have a $1.00 fixed value. Thus, all money market funds have the same NAV. We shall discuss what are called *loads* later. The point here is that money market funds are what are called *no load* funds. Since their general purpose is to hold money for a short period of time, and since their return is low compared with other mutual funds, there would be no way for a sales commission (i.e., load) to be made up.

There is a special kind of money market fund which is sometimes referred to as a *tax-free money market fund*. Such funds have an additional objective, which is to invest only in municipal bonds because income from municipal bonds is not subject to federal income tax. People in a high income tax bracket may find these money market funds attractive. It is counterproductive to invest in tax-free funds in a 403(b) retirement savings plan or IRAs or SRAs because they are already protected from current income taxes. However, when you take the money out, you will have to pay taxes on what should be tax-free income. There are also special tax-free money market funds which invest in the municipal instruments of only one state, so that people who pay income taxes in that state can avoid both state and federal income taxes on that money. There are even funds which confine themselves to Los Angeles or to New York City municipal instruments so that residents of those cities can avoid city, state, and federal income taxes on that money.

CREF offers a money market fund which is not a tax-free fund. Thus far, participants do not use the CREF Money Market Account for money from outside CREF or TIAA. If you decide to withdraw your TIAA money over their mandatory ten-year period, the CREF Money Market Account might be a good place to put the funds until you decide what else to do with them.

Fixed-Income Funds

These funds take a longer view of investments than the money market funds, and they invest primarily in bonds. Some fixed-income funds are invested only in notes and bonds of the federal government, and they are referred to as government funds. Such government funds are the most conservative of these funds. Since the federal government has the right to print money, its notes and bonds are free of risk as to the underlying principal. However, most fixed-income mutual funds invest in bonds of the federal government as well as what are called *investment grade* or *high-quality* corporate bonds. The theory is that while adding corporate bonds to the portfolio increases the risk, it also should increase income without substantially threatening the safety of the fund's principal.

CREF has recently established a fixed-income fund which they call their Bond Market Account. It has not been in existence long enough to be able to evaluate it by way of comparison to other fixed-income funds. However, given the general strength of CREF's investing in other areas, it is worth watching and keeping under consideration for use as part of your diversification in the fixed-income portion of your portfolio.

In the section on money market funds, there was a discussion of municipal money markets. There also are municipal bond funds which take a longer investment time horizon. They have the advantage of yielding income which is primarily exempt from federal income taxes. However, you need to be a little cautious here. Sometimes people who invest in a municipal bond fund expect to pay no federal income taxes at all on any returns from the fund. Income which is attributable to the interest on the bonds is exempt from federal income taxes. However, if the fund has a capital gain on the value of the underlying bonds, that income will be passed on to the investor, who must pay income tax on it. As is the case with tax-free money market funds, there are municipal bond funds for states and cities which free the shareholder from federal, state, and city income taxes on interest gained by. Once again, in general, they are not appropriate places for 403(b) money (i.e., defined-contribution retirement savings) or IRAs and SRAs.

■ *High-Yield Funds/Junk Bond Funds* A considerable amount of popular press attention has been given to what are called *junk bonds*. The earlier description of fixed-income mutual funds stated that such mutual funds invested in investment grade, high-quality bonds. Junk bonds are, by definition, bonds which are deemed to be less than investment grade. They are riskier both in terms of safety of principal and in terms of the ability to meet interest payments. Soon after junk bonds became popular, mutual funds which specialized in junk bonds were created. Those funds are sometimes known as *junk bond funds*, or, in less pejorative terms, *high-yield* funds. The yields on the junk bonds are usually considerably greater than those on investment grade bonds to make up for the increased risk. High-yield mutual funds were a less risky way to invest in junk bonds because they provided diversification among many issues. High-yield bond funds enjoyed a period of popularity, and then became unpopular as some corporations which had used junk bonds for capital could not meet the interest or principal payments. By and large, such funds remain unpopular as this book is being prepared, though the attitude may be starting to move in the other direction.

Equity Funds

These funds invest in a variety of stocks. Some funds may stick to specific criteria; for example, they may invest only in stocks listed on the New York Stock Exchange. Such a restriction helps reduce volatility because in general it is easier to sell listed securities than to sell unlisted, over-the-counter securities. Some funds invest primarily in the stock of large corporations. Some invest primarily in the stock of small, growing corporations. Some emphasize a set of related businesses or industries. Some emphasize regional interests. Some invest in stocks which traditionally pay generous dividends. Some invest in stocks which pay little in the way of dividends in the hope that the appreciation of the stock will make up for the lack of dividend. Since there are over one thousand equity mutual funds, as you narrow your choices of funds in accordance with the processes to be suggested, you should be able to find a number of funds which meet your personal objectives for growth-oriented equity investments.

Balanced Funds

These funds own both bonds and stocks. The managers of the funds make decisions as to whether the fund should be more heavily weighted toward stocks or bonds or cash equivalents. Perhaps the best way to think of them is as a university endowment. Typically, they are "prudently" run (i.e., they do not take risks which could not be defended as appropriate for people who seek the preservation of the capital and do not wish to assume a high degree of risk). Since I have suggested that the proper balance between fixed-income investments and stocks in a person's portfolio is, to a significant extent, related to the age, health, and risk aversion of the person, I do not think balanced funds are in general appropriate for individual portfolios. I believe these funds make more sense for portfolios such as college endowments, where the age and health factors are not relevant.

Index Funds

Index funds are of particular interest to participants in TIAA-CREF because the CREF Stock Account is a stock fund which is predominantly an index fund. Thus, if you have a significant portion of your retirement savings in the CREF Stock Account, you already own a portion of an index fund. Stock index funds attempt to imitate the actions of the broad stock market, so that they are neither very far ahead or very far behind the market, insuring the investors of an average performance.

Indexing is, ideally, a computer-based set of actions. Consider, for example, the most popular indexing, and the one which the CREF Stock Fund uses: indexing to the Standard and Poor's 500 Stock Index. The elements of that index are well known. The managers program a computer so that it will cause the holdings in the index fund to reflect as accurately as possible the S&P 500. There may be some lag in the process, and thus some inefficiencies, but they should be able to track reasonably closely. In practice, the process is more complicated than I have just suggested, but there is no reason for it to be much more complicated.

Indexing is often referred to as *passive* investing in contrast to *active* investment management, in which investment managers, backed by investment research staffs, comb through the relevant literature, visit the managements of companies, and perform mathematical analyses. Such active investment managers make judgments about what stocks will be in favor or out in the future. The managers then put their reputations on the line by buying or selling the issues.

In contrast, index investing requires no extensive research (except, perhaps, in computer programming), and the so-called managers should be able to sit back and watch as the computer program attempts to get the fund to imitate the market. The S&P 500 is not the only index which can be used. There are also bond indexes, and there are funds which are indexed to the bond index. There is a small-company stock index, and there are some funds indexed to the small-company index. As this appendix is being written, Standard and Poor's has announced that it is going to publish an S&P 400, which will be an index of mid-sized corporations. Almost surely by the time this book is published, there will be funds indexed to the S&P 400.

There should be a benefit from all indexing. The expenses of indexed funds should be substantially lower than the expenses of actively managed funds. After all, the managers do not have to make any substantial decisions. In fact, in the hierarchy of importance, the computer analysts should be paid the most. The managers hardly have to come to work. However, that has not followed thus far. We shall discuss the issue of fund expenses more completely later. In the preparation of this book, I examined over two hundred actively managed stock mutual funds. I also examined about twenty index stock funds. The mean expense ratio of the index funds was 0.91%. The mean expense ratio of the actively managed funds was 1.06%. These numbers alone give some indication of how small the difference is.

I cannot explain why the expenses of index funds are so high. I have studied prospecti to see if I can account for this phenomenon, but I cannot. If I had access to more internal data, I would look at the way in which expenses are allocated in fund families, which is where the index funds I examined are located. The expenses of the family structure may be allocated across all funds on some formulaic basis developed by cost accountants. If so, there may be expenses in there which are assigned to the index fund but which are not actually traceable to that fund.

Specialty Funds

As the name implies, specialty funds specialize in particular areas. There are funds which specialize in one industrial sector, in regions of the United States, in regions of the world, in small companies, funds in gold, funds in bankrupt companies, and so on. The list is almost endless. This is an area which may be useful for specific exploration because we may be able to use our scholarly knowledge in selecting a fund. From publishing to technology to economic trends to regional developments, there may be cases in which we can apply our knowledge to selecting a portion of our investments. Specialized mutual funds may present that opportunity while maintaining a measure of safety through the diversification in the fund structure itself, even though the fund may be specialized. Once again, the wisdom of allowing us to make our own decisions about where our retirement savings are invested is borne out.

Specialty funds may also be useful if you find some area of diversification is not covered. For example, many advisers suggest that at least a small portion of one's retirement savings should be in gold. I am not one of them, but if you are convinced by such advice, there are mutual funds which specialize in gold.

Ethical-Objectives Funds

The title is mine, and at the end of this section, I shall explain why I have selected it. There is no commonly accepted designation for this area. CREF, which has a new fund in this area, calls it the Social Choice Account. Fundamentally, the approach of these funds is to apply so-called ethical standards to the investment choices. In a sense, these funds are all specialty funds, and they might have been included under that heading. However, the issue of ethical investing may be of such special interest to academics that it is being treated separately here.

Thus far, the objectives of the ethical funds are based primarily on negatives: no nuclear power; no tobacco; no liquor; no organizations which support abortions; no weapons manufacturers; no South African investments (unless perhaps the corporation has adopted the Sullivan Principles); no Northern Ireland investments (unless perhaps the corporation has adopted the MacBride Principles), and so on. As far as I know, there are no funds which adopt all of the above negatives in their objectives, but most of them adopt at least some.

Complexities arise immediately. First, some of the specific objectives of particular funds might conflict with the views of a potential participant. For example, an individual might be opposed to investing in liquor but in favor of the right of women to choose an abortion. There probably are not many people who adopt all the negative positions listed above, and it is only a partial list.

Second, the very nature of the economy makes such decisions difficult if not impossible. Consider, for example, someone who is opposed to investing in organizations which are involved in nuclear power. It is reasonably easy to identify the manufacturers who make nuclear power generators and to avoid investing in them. However, how should the fund treat secondary sources which may be even more important? For example, should the fund avoid investments in banks which give lines of credit to the manufacturers of nuclear power? Should the fund avoid investing in financial services corporations which sponsor a family of mutual funds some of which invest in stocks of manufacturers of nuclear power? The answers are not easy. In many regards, the line of credit from a bank or the purchase of a new issue of securities by a fund may be more important to the fiscal health of the corporation than an individual decision to buy a few hundred shares of stock in the company. Since the market is pretty efficient, the probability is that if one person does not make the investment, someone else will. If there is any difference in the price which results from an individual's refusal to purchase those shares, it lies in an area logicians call *counterfactual conditionals,* which are notoriously difficult to assess. They make wonderful grist for dormitory bull sessions because they are almost entirely unresolvable. If there is a lesson which an individual hopes the management of a corporation will learn as a result of his or her refusal to purchase the stock, it will probably be lost on the management, not because management is malevolent, but because it will not see the effect. The economy is very intertwined and complex, and while some isolated actions can be taken, once there is any complication added, it will be difficult to carry out the proscriptions.

In my own view, ethical-objectives investments should be based more on positive, not negative, purposes. It would be exciting to put together a fund with an objective of investing in companies seeking alternative, nondestructive energy sources. My college physics tells me that solar energy and its variations wait upon the invention of an economical way to produce it massively. That does not mean it is easy, but it does mean that there are enormous potential rewards available to a corporation which solves that problem. As with environmental issues, so too, with serious medical issues. Consider, for example, an ethical-objective fund investing in companies which are concentrating on curing AIDS. Many investigators and inventors lack the capital resources to follow their visions and dreams. Admittedly, some of them are merely quacks, and surely any fund should try to avoid the quacks, but there are others who are challenging conventional wisdom and who, with adequate support, might find the solutions. An investment in such funds might simultaneously accomplish the negative (i.e., that money would *not* be going into support for offensive industries), and something positive (i.e., the solution sought might in fact come to pass), and *might* prove to be a worthwhile investment from a financial point of view. Historically, there is considerable evidence that many major break-throughs come not from further applications of conventional wisdom but from those who stand outside the mainstream. There is reason to suspect that conventional wisdom will continue to support con-ventional activities in conventional ways, and that at least some of the solutions to problems which seem so intractable will come from people dismissed as at least eccentric if not crazy. This is a perfect opportunity for socially responsible investment with defined ethi-cal objectives. Unfortunately, I know of no funds which specialize in this way. I hope they will come along. In the meantime, there is the range of "negative" ethical-objectives funds, and they, too, can be investigated.

There is a legitimate concern with the prospect of the positive ethical-objective funds that I suggest. It is that such funds may be so narrow as to diminish diversification and increase risk unacceptably. As I indicated earlier, ethical-objectives funds, whether they are of the negative or the positive variety, are best understood as specialty funds. Diversification could be achieved by investing in a number of such funds, and from a personal financial planning perspective, one should still continue diversification in other kinds of funds.

Having presented this classification of mutual funds, I turn to the topic of selecting appropriate mutual funds for a particular portfolio. That means that it will be important to have some processes which will enable you to sort through the variety of alternatives in order to select the ones which are most appropriate for you.

Narrowing the Field and Selecting Specific Funds

While the information about funds in general may seem to make the selection process more complex and difficult, it is possible to suggest some steps which will help narrow the alternatives to a manageable number for more thorough investigation. Ultimately, there is no sub-stitute for research, but we have been trained in the techniques of research, and if you adopt the suggestions made here, you will not find the amount of research to be onerous. The initial steps do not in-volve making investment analysis judgments, and by the time such judgments are called for, the lists should be small.

Objectives

The previous section outlined the varied objectives of mutual funds. There are many funds with objectives which will not fit yours. For example, you will probably not find investment in tax-free funds advisable for your IRAs, SRAs or 403(b) retirement savings. This one criterion eliminates almost 50% of the money market funds and 50% of the fixed-income funds. I have also suggested that there is little reason for you to own balanced funds.

The broadest differentiation between funds is between fixed-income funds (which includes money market funds) and equity funds. You will want to make your own decisions about using index funds, specialty funds, and ethical-objectives funds, most of which are equity funds. I have already suggested how you might decide on the issue of allocation between fixed income and equity. Thus, identifying your own objectives will eliminate many funds, and it is a reasonable first step.

Longevity of Fund

A second reasonable criterion for fund selection is to eliminate from consideration all those funds which do not have a track record sustained over a significant period of time. My own research shows that about one-quarter of the fixed-income funds and about one-half of the equity funds have been in existence for less than five years. In making a first pass at narrowing the field, it makes sense to eliminate them on the grounds that you will not have enough data to tell how they have done under varying economic and market conditions.[1]

Fund Family

A third criterion is to eliminate those funds which are not part of what is called a *family* of funds. The designation of family means that the fund is part of an investment management organization which sponsors a number of mutual funds. My own research does not show that historically funds in families have done noticeably better than independent funds. However, fund families do offer a benefit which is significant. They allow for considerable ease of transfer of money within the particular family. The family feature allows you to move your investments within the family, often with little more than a telephone call. That may be important to you as you decide to re-allocate your portfolio with advancing years or as you may change your own investment views. If you transfer funds out of a family or from one independent fund into another, you will have more paper-work which will have to be completed within sixty days. That is not an insurmountable barrier, and it is certainly not a good reason for avoiding a transfer when that makes financial sense, but there are benefits in ease of transfer. In addition, I have found that there may be a slight service edge to the family funds over the independent funds.

In sum, since there is no performance edge which I can identify for independent versus family funds, I suggest that there is something of an edge for the families; thus, in the first pass for narrowing your choice, it makes sense to stay with the family funds.

Loads

The topic of what are called *loads* for mutual funds has been made more confusing than it needs to be. Broadly speaking, there used to be two kinds of open-end mutual funds: load and no-load. The word *load* is a euphemism for "commission."

The first confusion enters right away in determining what the load—the commission—is. The mutual fund industry says one thing, but an objective analysis indicates something else. If we go through a typical calculation, it will be easier to understand the issues. As this is being written, I have looked at a particular mutual fund which, in the interest of reinforcing the no-conflicts-of-interest approach, I shall not name, but I shall use its actual numbers. The newspaper shows what is called an "offer price" of $10.95 per share for this mutual fund. It also shows the net asset value of the mutual fund to be $10.02. What that means is that if you wish to purchase a share of the mutual fund, you will pay $10.95 for each share, but the share you will receive is actually worth only $10.02. So, what is the commission? (I know this sounds like fourth-grade arithmetic, but you may be surprised at the answer.) Let's take $10.95 and subtract $10.02 to arrive at 93 cents, which is the per share commission. On that issue, everyone agrees, so we are ready for the next question:

What is the commission percentage? That seems to be easy: divide 0.93 by 10.02. The answer is 9.28% or, rounded off, 9.3%. *However,* that is not what the mutual fund industry says it is. *They* take the same 0.93 and divide it by 10.95 to arrive at 8.49% or, rounded off, 8.5%. The mutual fund industry has people who are willing to defend stubbornly the notion that 8.5% is the accurate percentage, but, of course, in order to get a $10.02 investment, you have to give an additional 93 cents.

As indicated, there were and are so-called no-load mutual funds. Originally, these meant exactly what they said: no commission is charged for purchasing a share in the mutual fund. Thus, when the investor purchases a share for $10.95, the NAV is also $10.95. The no-load funds are indicated by NL under the offer price in the paper.

These reasonably clear distinctions have been further confused. The load mutual funds found themselves under heavy competition from the no-load mutual funds. There is no solid evidence that load funds in general outperform no-load funds in general and even less solid evidence that they perform sufficiently well to make up for the commission. Thus, load funds began to moderate their commissions. We now have full-load funds, mid-load funds, low-load funds, and no-load funds. The designations are not clear, though there is some talk of the SEC trying to restrict the designation of *low-load* to those which charge 3% or less (using the industry's method of calculation), and *no-load* to funds which do not charge any load. You should calculate the load if you consider investing in funds which charge a load. Your investment's performance will have to be that much better to offset the cost of the load.

If the NAV number and the offer price number are the same and there is no NL in the listing, the fund probably has what is called a redemptive, or exit, load; that is, under some circumstances you will have to pay something extra upon selling your shares. If you decide to investigate such funds, it will be important for you to examine these provisions. Sometimes the exit load is on a declining time scale, so that after a period of time there will be no exit load. The purpose of a declining exit load may be to discourage short-term traders from using the fund, and that may be advantageous to the long-term traders such as you because servicing short-term trades is expensive administratively and can be disruptive to systematic investment management. If you intend to leave your money in the fund beyond the duration of the period, a declining-time-scale redemptive fee should not be a barrier. If you intend to get out in a shorter period of time, it may pose a barrier. Some funds do not have a declining time scale on their exit load, and in any event, it is important to remember that the exit load will be charged on the NAV the fund has achieved *at the time you sell*, not at the time you bought. Since we all hope the NAV at the time you sell is higher than at the time you bought, that means the dollar amount will be higher than an equivalent percentage on entry. Some funds even give investors a choice as to whether they would rather pay the commission at the beginning or the end (which always reminded me of choosing between death by electrocution or by lethal injection).

Some advisers suggest eschewing all funds which charge a load or a redemption fee. That is another way to narrow the field quickly. However, I think that while the effect of loads should always be taken into account in comparing one fund with another, using such a broad brush may force you to leave out too many funds which may be appropriate in spite of their loads.

Of course, money market funds do not charge a load. With regard to fixed-income funds, you might consider all those with no loads and some of those with low loads. After all, if a 3% low-load, fixed-income fund is held for six years, it only has to do 0.5% better per year in interest to equal a no-load fund. Also, in the case of fixed-income funds, it might be wise to include funds which charge redemption fees if the fees are on a rapidly declining time scale. However, it is important to recall that each percentage point which goes to the fund is one point less for *your* interest, and, if your analysis makes other factors equal, you should select the pure no-load fund. In regard to equity funds, you might relax even further strictures on loads, though it is unlikely that the full load of 9.3% will be justified. As a first pass, you might look at growth-oriented equity funds which have an actual load of approximately 4.5% (the industry will call it a 4% load). The purpose of the equity fund is to earn a significant total return, which includes dividends as well as capital gains. Thus, improved performance *may* be able to overwhelm the commission charged. Again, what you are looking for is total return net of any commission, and the higher the load, the more difficult it will be for the fund to make the target. There is no evidence I know of that there is a correlation (direct or inverse) between load charged and investment success. I have run the statistical analyses for some years, and I find none among the funds I follow. However, that does not mean that if you find a load fund which you are convinced will prove to be very positive, and there is no equivalent in a no-load form, you should turn down the load fund just because it charges a load.

12b-1 Fees

As if understanding loads were not confusing enough, there are more indirect methods for passing costs along to the investors. As you examine the mutual fund listing in the papers, you will see a *p* next to some listings for both load and no-load mutual funds. That symbol means that the fund referenced applies costs covered under what is called the *12b-1 plan*. Curiously, an announced theory of the 12b-1 plan was to help no-load mutual funds with their marketing costs and to give them ways to entice brokers and others to recommend no-load funds to their customers. 12b-1 plans often include provisions for salespeople to receive what are called *trail fees*, which pay as long as customers do not redeem their shares. In my view, funds which use 12b-1 fees should not be listed as no-load funds, but the SEC thus far has not so ruled.

In the preparation of this book, I analyzed data for about two thousand mutual funds. Almost two-thirds of the load funds I analyzed also charge 12b-1 fees. However, less than one-fourth of the no-load funds also charge 12b-1 fees. (The exact numbers are as follows: Of 1,365 load funds, 889 also charge 12b-1 fees. Of 635 no-load funds, 143 charge 12b-1 fees.) It is ironic that what was started as an attractive situation for the no-load funds has been absorbed by funds that charge a load. Since there is no evidence I know of to indicate that funds which take advantage of 12b-1 plans do any better than those which do not, I would eliminate them in the first pass at narrowing the list of funds to those which should be considered carefully. Another device for absorbing high management and marketing costs has been to pack the costs into the expenses of the mutual fund itself. However, in order to identify those costs, you will have to read a prospectus, and at this stage of selection, I have not suggested that you ask for prospecti.

Asset Size

Another criterion which might be used in selecting funds relates to the total asset size of the fund. In general, especially with regard to equity funds, a very large fund may have a difficult time responding to changes in the market without causing problems for itself. Investment changes other than marginal ones need to be planned far ahead of time and can be executed only over time. That means the fund may not be able to respond rapidly to new circumstances. Among equity funds, this is more of a problem for the actively managed funds than for the passive index funds. The managed funds are attempting to do better than the index, and, in order to do so, they must move in significant ways. Excessive size may be counterproductive. At the same time, if a fund is too small, it may not be able to diversify sufficiently, and it may have to maintain a disproportionately high cash reserve to cover potential shareholder redemptions. For example, I have read about one mutual fund with just over $100,000 in assets. In my view, that is too small to be effective and provide the appropriate diversification.

For the purposes of this book, I examined growth-oriented equity funds. In accordance with the selection criteria suggested above, I eliminated those with less than a five-year track record, those outside a family, those with loads above 4.5%, and those with 12b-1 fees. That left me with twenty-seven candidates. Their assets ranged from just about $17 million to over $12 billion. The median asset size was slightly over $1 billion. Sixteen of the twenty-seven funds had assets between approximately $100 million and $1 billion. My suggestion is to use that range as another criterion for narrowing your choice of an equity fund. In that way, you can be assured that your fund is large enough to have the advantages of diversification and yet small enough to be able to be able to respond to anticipated changes in the market. (It may give you some sense of the size of the CREF Stock Account to note that the twenty-seven funds referred to included the largest single mutual fund, and even so, the *total* assets of all those funds do not equal those of the CREF Stock Account alone.)

The situation is somewhat different in the case of fixed-income mutual funds. In that case, using the selection principles articulated thus far, the funds themselves tend to be smaller, and there is perhaps less reason to be concerned with excessive size. The purpose of

the funds is not so much to respond rapidly to the investment manager's expectation of the direction of the market as to preserve capital
and deliver a reliable investment income to the shareholders. I would
suggest the same bottom limit of $100 million for the fixed-income
fund, and no effective top limit. Once again, for the purposes of this
book, I first narrowed the list in accordance with the earlier criteria suggested and then included the suggested asset size criterion.
That process yielded twenty-six fixed-income mutual funds. Their
median size was about $500 million. The assets of the largest fixed-
income mutual fund that I know about are approximately $11 billion.
The *total* assets of these twenty-six funds are less than the assets of
TIAA alone.

With regard to money market funds, once again, I would be cautious about those with assets significantly less than $25 million.
However, my primary criterion would be whether there are money
market funds in the different families of funds with which you are
working. In the next sections, I shall discuss other criteria which
might be applied to the analysis of all funds, but at this point, con-
venience would be most important to me. In general, money market
fund managers do not try to play the market as aggressively as equity
fund managers may. Their purpose is to keep a very liquid fund responsive to purchases and sales of the fund shares. Since the fund
will use very liquid investment instruments, and since those will be
turning over frequently, redeeming shares on demand should not be
difficult.

The next step in narrowing the list of prospective funds takes you
to reading the prospecti. That is done much too infrequently in part,
I suspect, because they seem daunting and in part because they seem
to be uninviting literature. However, with some guidance, I believe
prospecti can be made intelligible.

How to Read a Prospectus

Now that you have a manageable number of prospective mutual fund
candidates, you are ready to request further information. The information should help you narrow the list even further. No matter what
you request, the information sent you will probably include some
glossy materials as well as a prospectus. By law, it *must* include a

prospectus before the company is permitted to ask you to complete an application to purchase shares. The earlier analogy to college admissions is still appropriate. No matter how insistently prospective students may ask for a catalogue, they are likely to receive what is called a *viewbook*. In fact, some colleges refuse to give prospective students a catalogue before they have had a viewbook.

Leaving aside the issue of a legal requirement, the analogy between the catalogue and the prospectus is apt. Both are written by professionals for professionals in professional language. Both are technical and forbidding. Both are poorly written and tend to confuse more than communicate. However, there is one difference. I think I can help people learn how to make sense out of a prospectus.

Some people worry about how they are going to get the literature on the funds. First, of course, I suggest talking to your reference librarian. There are sources of data which are not merely covers for selling. There are services which the librarians will know about. Those services will give some elementary descriptions and data about mutual funds, and you can use some of that data in your earliest efforts at narrowing the list. You will also find that the vast majority of funds—and all fund families I know about—have toll-free numbers. A telephone call will get you a quick response. I assume many of the funds sell their mailing lists, and your name will be there as a prospect. Once you start, your mailbox is likely to look like those of high school seniors who have high achievement examination scores.

In a sense, this is another research project, and the standard canons of proper research are appropriate. Many academics may find the literature boring when it is not downright offensive from a literary perspective, but we all examine lots of unexciting material in the course of doing scholarly research. Administrative reports and academic journals are hardly paragons of linguistic virtue.

The slick brochures will be written to satisfy a marketing and public relations plan for the fund. That does not mean they should not be read. Like the university viewbook, which is certainly worth viewing, the public relations pieces should be read carefully for information which you may wish to examine in more depth through reading the prospectus.[2]

The prospectus is basically written to satisfy requirements of the Securities and Exchange Commission. The purpose is not to communicate clearly and accurately to a normal person. You will have to search to find the truth in these documents. Philosophy faculty call this unpacking; linguistic faculty call it searching for hidden meanings; foreign-language faculty call it translating. Lawyers call it good English. Whatever background you bring to it, no doubt part of your task as a scholar is to search for something which is not obvious. That is true here, too.

There is a great deal in prospecti which you do not need to read with much care, and after reading a few, you will soon learn that much of it is boilerplate. However, there is worthwhile information which you should be able to discover rapidly and to which you should give your attention.

One of the first things to do in reading the prospectus is to notice the date. While the funds are usually good about sending recent copies, it is useful to know how dated the prospectus is. A second thing to do is to check information which you already think you know in regard to the fund. Read carefully the description of its stated objectives and be sure that is what you want. Funds have mechanisms for changing objectives, though that usually requires approval of shareholders. It is possible that between the time you read about a fund and the time you are prepared to invest in it, the objective has changed. Verify your understanding of the age of the fund by looking at its performance data and checking to be sure it is at least the five years you sought (if you follow the earlier suggestion). Some care should be exercised here. Occasionally, a fund will present its data in order to give the impression that the fund has been in existence for a considerable period of time, but when you check closely you find a footnote indicating the comparative data is "since inception" rather than for a five-year period. Be sure to read the section on sales commissions, redemption fees, exit fees, and so forth. Funds will present the information, but they do not all like to present it clearly and carefully. Look for 12b-1 charges or the right to charge them if management should decide to do so. Check to be sure the size of the fund is within the ranges you established. You might also look to see if there have been any sudden changes in asset size. If so, that is a red flag. If a substantial portion of the investors are using a fund for "timing" purposes, the expenses of the fund can run up quickly, and the volatility of the NAV may be high. A reasonable and steady increase in fund size is generally a good sign. The prospectus should reveal the extent of the family connections of the fund. You should look for ease of transfer within the family; some funds will allow telephone transfer with a paper back-up to follow; you should determine whether there are sales charges to be paid if you move from one fund to another, and you should determine whether there is a money market fund as part of the family. You should look at the ease with which the fund will set up 403(b)(7) accounts, IRAs and roll-over IRAs. Once you have checked on this information, you are ready to make some further selections based upon information you may discover in the prospecti.

Expense Ratios

You should be able to find information about what is called the fund's *expense ratio*. The expense ratio is calculated by dividing the fund's average net assets for a period of time into its expenses for that same period. The expense ratio gives you an indication of the cost of managing the fund. Other things being equal, of course, you would rather have a low expense ratio than a high one, but other things usually are not actually equal, and that guide is probably too general. In general, fixed-income funds should have lower expense ratios than equity funds; index funds *should* have low expense ratios; actively managed equity funds (i.e., those which are not indexed) may have higher expense ratios, and the specialty funds probably will have the highest. (There are not enough ethical-objective funds for me to feel comfortable with constructing averages in that case.) There are, however, many exceptions to each of these generalizations, and it is important to look at each situation carefully, remembering that expenses can eat up your gains.

For first-analysis purposes, I would suggest using the following expense ratios as maxima. They are close to the median in each class when including only those funds which fit the criteria already suggested.

Fixed Income: 0.75%
Actively managed Equity: 1.25%
Specialty: 1.75%
Index: 0.75%

The median expense ratio for index funds, within the other constraints suggested, is actually 1.00%. However, a ratio that high for an index fund makes no sense to me relative to actively managed funds. Thus, I suggest using 0.75% as a maximum. I think it should be much lower, and this is a compromise with reality, but competition may drive this maximum down. In my view, there really is no excuse for such extraordinary expenses associated with an index fund. Some index funds, including, to their credit, the CREF Stock Account, have ratios well below the maximum I have suggested.

You should not assume that all expense ratios are about the same. Of funds I have examined, the range runs from over 9.00% to 0.00%. In addition, do not be fooled by 0.00% expense ratios. A fund cannot be operated without any expenses. Typically, funds with 0.00% expense ratios are new funds trying to lure customers. Management usually has some latitude for setting the expenses charged to shareholders. They may be trying a variation of the bait-and-switch financial aid game which is pursued by some universities. You should read the provisions for changes in expense ratios and chargeable expenses carefully to determine what constraints there are on management. In addition, you might look at the historical pattern, and at the pattern of other funds in the family. There is a noticeable clustering of expense ratios among families. Some families tend to have high ratios; some tend to cluster toward the median and some tend to have low ratios. If you find a fund with a 0.00% ratio which is being sponsored by one of the families which tend to have high ratios, you can expect that after the initial offerings, the ratio will rise. The clustering of expense ratios increases my suspicion that there is considerable discretion in the expense side of these funds and that assigned expenses for an individual fund are, to a considerable extent, controllable by management. Without adequate numbers, I cannot test my suspicion in regard to index funds, but that is my best preliminary explanation for the fact that their ratios remain inexplicably high.

My guess is that family managements are using some of their funds as what are called *cash cows*. I suspect they use them to generate money supposedly for expenses, but that money is diverted to developing and supporting other funds.

It is important to remember that the expense ratio, unlike the load, is a continuing charge, not a one-time charge. Thus, it is a constant drain on your annual earnings, and the fund will have to work even harder to compensate for it. That is my reason for suggesting that you examine only those which fall below the median in the class. No evidence I know of shows that there is a correlation between expense ratios and performance.

If you have followed the advice suggested above, you should have narrowed your list of funds to a very small number and have been able to read through the prospecti reasonably quickly. You have done all this without making any judgments about investment management.

Performance

You are now ready for a more complete analysis of the prospecti. At this stage, I think a close reading is in order. I look at the calculations of past performance. Since you are looking at funds with at least a five-year track record, you should get some information from that. There will probably be a warning indicating that the past is not predictive of the future. That is, of course, true, but you may use it as some indication as to how well management has done in the past. It makes sense to me to put more faith in managers who have had better performances in the past. You should be able to compare the performance records of the few funds you are considering seriously.

In addition to performance data, I try to examine what I can of the fund's management and management style. For example, I am more impressed with fund managers who regularly visit the management of the corporations. That is something you and I cannot do. I believe in primary research in this field as I do in my own. I also look at discussions of family fund relationships to attempt to detect whether the fund I am examining is one of the family's cash cows.

I look at stability of portfolio management. While I have said repeatedly that there is no evidence I know that portfolio managers can consistently do better than the averages, I grow concerned when they change often. Each changeover may be a time when the new people think they must put their stamp on the fund and take responsibility for the fund's direction. Such activities may result in increased transaction costs as holdings are sold and bought in an effort to reorient the fund.

After you have read a fund's prospectus, you should feel free to call the fund and ask questions. If you keep asking questions and do not receive useful answers, keep pressing until you find someone who will answer your question. Your questions should be respected by the people at the fund. In most cases, I have found them cooperative and helpful even when the question was embarrassing to them. They usually want to answer questions because, if they refuse to answer, they will have virtually guaranteed the loss of a customer, whereas if they answer, they may gain a customer. Do not invest until you are satisfied. If you do not get satisfactory answers, cross that fund off your list. There will be more funds. It is rare to find a situation in which you cannot find alternative funds of near to equal value, and you are under no obligation to force the fund to do the work it should be doing already. After you have answers to all your questions, you will already be among a small class of mutual fund investors who do their homework, and you should be ready to make your decisions with more confidence. If the selection process has worked as I intend, you will be selecting from among a number of appropriate funds, so your eventual specific selections should not be dangerously risky. Presumably, you will be diversifying among funds and fund families, so you will not have to narrow your selection down to a single fund.

Market Timing and Dollar-Cost Averaging

Since presumably you have made some decisions about which funds you wish to invest in, the next step is to make the actual investments. There are people who believe that while we cannot hope to call the movements of individual securities accurately, we should be able to predict broad swings in the economy in general and in the market in particular. Thus, they advise timing investments so that they are purchased at the bottom and sold at the top. As with the horse track, there are many people out there writing newsletters and giving advice in other ways. For a hefty price, they will make the predictions for you. However, there is a considerable difference between fortune telling and accurate predictions. As far as I know, no one has yet been able to call major changes in the market accurately even three times in a row. Beyond that, even for those who may claim to have done so, as intellectuals we would insist on another element: that there be a theoretical base from which the predictions are made and that the theoretical base be sufficient for deriving the predictions. As far as I know, there is no such capacity. I have studied finance for about thirty years, and, while there was some considerable optimism about this prospect when I started, events of the intervening years seem to have dashed realistic hopes.

Once again, there is a way around this problem. One does not have to pretend to be a market prognosticator. The procedure suggested here is known as dollar-cost averaging, and (like prose) TIAA-

CREF participants have been using it all along without knowing it. Our retirement funds are invested in TIAA-CREF through dollar-cost averaging. What that means is that we invest approximately the same amount of money at regular periods of time. The theory behind dollar-cost averaging is twofold: first, we *cannot* predict the markets accurately; second, if we dollar-cost average, we shall buy more shares when the price is down and, of course, fewer shares when the price is high. In a sense, dollar-cost averaging is a way of achieving diversification over time, while purchasing mutual fund shares helps achieve diversification instantly. If the underlying long-term trend of the market is positive, the result for the investor will be positive irrespective of temporary rises and falls. Neither dollar-cost averaging nor the process of selecting mutual funds that I have suggested is magic. Each of these strategies carries an element of risk, as does every other strategy. The element of risk cannot be eliminated. However, I hope the processes I have suggested will help minimize it and help you understand your alternatives.

Recently, Michael Edelson has suggested another way of diversifying over time. He calls it *value averaging*, and he indicates that his research shows that it achieves superior results. It is somewhat more complicated to administer than dollar-cost averaging, but for those willing to make the extra effort, it may be worthwhile. I can only explain it briefly here. If you are interested, I suggest you read Edelson's book carefully. Let us take a simple example. Suppose you had decided to follow dollar-cost averaging and put a set amount of money every other week into a particular mutual fund. Edelson would suggest that instead of depositing a set amount of money, you should adjust that so you are investing a set amount of value. When the growth of the fund is strong, you count its growth in with your contribution so that they are balanced out. Thus, you make a smaller contribution. When the fund's pricing is weak, assuming you have faith in the management of the fund, you invest more than you might have otherwise. I have stated this imprecisely, but Edelson suggests precise formulae for you to follow.[3] As I read it, value averaging exaggerates the effects of dollar-cost averaging.

Insofar as possible, it is advisable to use the principle of dollar-cost averaging or value averaging as you move your assets around among funds and as you change your allocation ratios, which is why planning is so important. Dollar-cost averaging and value averaging are not only good policies for investment purposes, they are also good policies for withdrawing funds from retirement savings.

Closed-End Mutual Funds

Closed-end mutual funds are in significant contrast to open-end funds. Perhaps the easiest way to understand a closed-end mutual fund is to imagine what it would be like to create one. Suppose a person who was a professional investment manager could convince others that he could do very well managing a mutual fund, though for reasons to be suggested later, he wanted to set up a closed-end mutual fund. He might go to prospective investors and persuade them to invest capital in the mutual fund he wanted to start. In return for their capital, they would receive shares in the mutual fund; that is, their shares would represent an undivided proportional interest in the mutual fund. Unlike the open-end mutual fund, these shares would be fixed in number. While original investors might sell their shares to someone else, new shares would not be created as demand for the mutual fund grew, nor would shares be redeemed as demand for the mutual fund declined. Essentially, the investors in the mutual fund would be investing in the investment management ability of the managers of the fund.

From a capital formation perspective, unlike the open-end mutual fund, the closed-end mutual fund operates like a standard business. The shares may be traded on one of the public stock exchanges, in the over-the-counter market, or they might be very closely held and traded only on a private basis. People who wish to purchase shares in the closed-end mutual fund do so in the open market. The investment managers of the closed-end mutual funds make their investments with the money in the fund. They manage the portfolio as the managers of a college endowment manage it, though they may not be as conservative.

Closed-end mutual funds have some advantages over open-end mutual funds. There is a tax advantage in closed-end mutual funds for investors using after-tax dollars. (These advantages do not apply to tax-sheltered plans.) In an open-end mutual fund, the investor has no choice about realizing gains for tax purposes; capital gains must be recognized each year for tax purposes. The closed-end mutual fund gives the investor more control over that situation because capital gains are not recognized and the corresponding taxes are not paid until the investor decides to sell the closed-end fund shares. That means the investor has more control over when the capital gains will be recognized and taxes paid.

Another potential advantage of closed-end mutual funds is that

there is hope that the stock will sell at a premium over the underlying value of the investments which are held in the fund. Call that
underlying value the *book value* of the mutual fund. The hope is
that the market value will be in excess of the book value. Unfortunately, closed-end funds usually sell at a discount to book value. Still
another advantage of closed-end mutual funds is that the managers
do not have to maintain cash reserves in case shareholders wish to
redeem their shares. Thus, all the money can be put to work, and the
fund should achieve maximum effectiveness.

I have not studied closed-end mutual funds in the breadth or depth
I have studied open-end mutual funds. Part of the reason is that there
does not seem to be convincing evidence that they do any better
than the open-end mutual funds. I have found them less customer
oriented, and I know of none which concentrate on 403(b) work. However, you may find them appropriate, and they can be analyzed in the
ways that open-end mutual funds can be analyzed. The fact that the
market typically sells closed-end mutual funds at a discount from
the value of their underlying securities tells me something about the
expectations of others for those funds.

Further Future Confusion

Many people familiar with mutual funds believe the SEC may be
preparing to make major recommendations in the near future with regard to mutual fund regulations. For example, I have already pointed
out the problems of open-end mutual funds in the face of a sudden
desire on the part of a large number of shareholders to withdraw their
money. The SEC is apparently considering approving some funds
operating with announced restrictions. For example, some funds
might allow the sale of their shares only once each month at a specified date. The times might be varied from fund to fund. In that way,
managers would have more ability to predict and manage the needs
of the fund—or, at least that is what the advocates of the changes
say. Another suggestion which has been discussed would simplify
the presentation of the numerous fees charged by the funds. Presumably, there would still be choice. Some funds might accept the new
provisions, and others might remain with the current situation.

The fact that the SEC may be considering reworking regulations
for the mutual fund industry (including CREF) means we shall have

to follow such developments carefully. Over the past years, the SEC has become more an extension of the financial services industry than an advocate for consumers. We shall have to watch on our own.

If this appendix has been successful, you should have already gained greater control over your own investments, and you should be able to make some specific investment decisions with some confidence. Once you have gone through the process a few times, I think you will find that it is not unduly burdensome. I would not suggest that anyone should attempt to accomplish all that is set out here at one time. It is sensible to absorb the information one step at a time. However, there is nothing about this world of investment management that you should not be able to understand.

Notes

Chapter 1. Orientation

1 Howard R. Bowen and Jack H. Schuster, *American Professors: A National Resource Imperiled* (New York: Oxford University Press, 1986), 263–64.
2 Ibid, 264.

Chapter 2. Sources of Advice

1 Teachers Insurance and Annuity Association/College Retirement Equities Fund, *Annual Report*, 2–3.
2 *The Chronicle of Higher Education*, March 20, 1991: A18.
3 "AAUP Chief Questions Pension Companies' Governance," *The Chronicle of Higher Education*, December 4, 1991: A25.

Chapter 3. Early Career and Early Preretirement Planning

1 Some people may regard this constraint as rather innocuous and uninteresting. They may reason that since they do not analyze the holdings in CREF accounts carefully now, they have no intention of analyzing the holdings in TIAA even if they were itemized. I think three points are worthy of consideration in this context. First, a few years ago, some knowledgeable academics and other members of the general investment community were critical of the performance of the CREF Stock Account. Subsequently, the executives of CREF changed the investment policy of CREF to its current one. While we need to be careful not to commit a *post hoc ergo propter hoc* fallacy, it is not unreasonable to suspect that some of the reason for the change in policy was the general criticism. Of course, neither knowledgeable academics nor the general investment community can evaluate the performance of an account if critical data is not available. Thus, there is not much they can say, and we can read, about the performance of TIAA. Second, it appears that the people in colleges and universities who led the efforts to force TIAA-CREF into transferability and cashability were inspired at least in part by the criticisms of CREF's investment performance. Finally, the most generous interpretation I can put on TIAA's continuing intransigence on this issue of full disclosure to us as its members is that the executives are being stubborn. Perhaps we cannot make the comparative analyses, but we might be edified by

215

such analyses done by professionals. We, the participants and members of TIAA, can have neither under current TIAA policies.

Chapter 4. Middle Career and Middle Preretirement Planning

1 For example, apparently the reason TIAA requires that individual withdrawals be accomplished over a ten-year period is that it is apprehensive about a possible run on TIAA funds and concerned that such a run might force it to sell some holdings at disadvantageous prices. However, if TIAA would tell participants the itemized current value of their funds, it *might* dispel any propensity to leave TIAA by showing that the funds are invested well and successfully and that TIAA constitutes at least as good a fixed-income investment as any alternative. Since TIAA continues to play hide-and-seek with our funds, it may encourage objective advisers, who, by definition, are not on the TIAA-CREF payroll, to suggest to us that we remove our funds—which is just the result they feared in the first place.

2 *The Wall Street Journal*, September 6, 1991: C1. I have thought of this situation when I have heard business executives berate the ineptitude of university faculty and argue that what is needed is a way to assess the value added by the faculty in teaching students. Theoretically, I concur, but I am always put in mind of Matthew 7:3: "Why beholdest thou the mote that is in thy brother's eye but considerest not the beam that is in thine own?" Surely, none of us settle for teaching which would be no better than that produced by computer-based averages, much less than that based on pure randomness.

3 It should be pointed out that the CREF Stock Account is not a *pure* index fund. Some elements are managed, but the basic thrust and investment strategy of the CREF Stock Account are those of an index fund.

4 When my wife and I were in the process of making such provisions for our children, we wanted to hear their response to the guardianship arrangements we were suggesting in the event of our death. However, we were very concerned about the psychological effects of discussing the possibility of our death with them. Thus, we approached the topic gingerly and cautiously. Once the children heard who their guardians would be, they seemed very happy, and it became clear that they were not at all traumatized. In fact, we thought their response was a little unseemly.

5 "Gnawing on Nest Eggs: Pensions at Risk," *Barron's*, December 2, 1991: 19.

Chapter 5. Late Career and Intensive Preretirement Planning

1 Actually, of course, it is all considerably more complicated. The estimates may vary, the insurance company will hold back some money to make

sure its estimates are correct, and the company will take out some money for the costs of operating the corporation. However, the point is to understand the principles of an annuity. Long before you purchase an annuity, you will need to ask those offering it to present you with some actual figures as to the payments.

Appendix: Personal Investment Management

1 It is important to emphasize that my suggestion is on the level of a first pass. I am *not* suggesting that such funds be eliminated from consideration entirely. For example, I have suggested that you might consider using the CREF Bond Market Account as part of your fixed-income portfolio. In addition, those who wish to use specialty funds and ethical-objectives funds will find that, in general, they tend to be younger. For example, as far as I can tell, there are about twenty-four funds which specialize in investments in what is loosely called the Pacific Rim. Of that number, I have only looked at about a dozen with any care, and of that dozen there are only six which have been in existence for five or more years. If you have a special interest in that area, you might wish to include additional funds with a shorter life, reasoning that your knowledge of the area in general can compensate for a lack of historical data about the fund itself.

2 Darrell Huff once wrote an amusing little book called *How to Lie with Statistics*. It is amusing in the spirit of Parkinson and others, teaching serious lessons through humor. Huff's book is a good antidote to reading the PR pieces and the prospecti of mutual funds. His chapter on the "Gee-Whiz Graph" is especially appropriate. See Darrell Huff, *How to Lie with Statistics* (New York: W. W. Norton, 1954).

3 See Michael Edelson, *Value Averaging: the Safe and Easy Strategy for Higher Investment Returns* (New York: International Publishers, 1990).

Index

AARP. *See* American Association of Retired Persons

Academic Professors. See Bowen and Schuster

Academic staff: mentioned, xiv–xv, xviii, 4, 7

Active investing: compared to passive investing, 192

Administration, college and university: mentioned, xiii–xiv

Administrative staff. *See* Academic staff

AIDS: mentioned, 195

Allocation of investments: based on age, 50, 52, 54, 121–22, 129, 146

American Association of Retired Persons: and reverse mortgages, 115

Annuity. *See* Annuities

Annuities: irreversible, 15, 146; TIAA–CREF, 16; radical changes, 16; for funding retirement, 92–99; variable annuity, 94; fixed annuity, 94; fixed period, 97; lifetime, 97; guaranteed period, 97; two–life, 98; single–life, 98; single–life with life insurance, 98; review by fee–only planner, 99; combined with self–management and age shift, 124; diversification of placement, 125; timing of payments, 125; mid–retirement years, 146–47; mentioned, 5, 128, 157, 216–17*n1*

Atwell, Robert: quoted, 25

Balanced mutual funds: described and discussed, 191

Barron's: referenced, 81; cited, 216*n5*

Benefit programs: cafeteria style, 89–90

Benefits officers, university: as source of information, 26; limitations, 26–27

Bowen, Howard R. *See* Bowen and Schuster

Bowen and Schuster: quoted on retirement, 6–7; cited, 215*n1*

Business: the study of, xii, xiii

By-Pass trust: for estate planning, 175

Carnegie, Andrew: mentioned, 5

Caducity: mentioned, 122

Cashability: at retirement, 3, 95, 123; and forward averaging, 127; mentioned, 215–16*n1*

Charitable remainder trusts: for estate planning, 175–76

Charitable remainder unitrusts: for estate planning, 176

Chronicle of Higher Education, The: cited, 215*nn2,3*; mentioned, 4, 25

"Churn and Burn": referenced, 99

Communities, lifetime care. *See* lifetime care communities

Conflict of interest: sales, 24

Corporate bonds: investment grade, 189

Counterfactual conditionals: mentioned, 195

CREF: bond market account, 50–51, 190; money market account, 52, 189; social choice account, 52, 194; stock account described and discussed, 61–62, 192–93, 202, 207; impact of size, 61–62; advantages in early career, 62; mentioned, 93, 212, 217*nn1,3*

Crummey trusts: for estate planning, 173

Custodial care health insurance: described and discussed, 154–56

Customer service representatives. *See* financial planners

De facto poverty: and medicaid planning, 150–54

De jure poverty: and medicaid planning, 151–54

219